TED STRONG JR.

TED STRONG JR.

The Untold Story of an Original Harlem Globetrotter and Negro Leagues All-Star

SHERMAN L. JENKINS

ROWMAN & LITTLEFIELD
Lanham • Boulder • New York • London

Published by Rowman & Littlefield
An imprint of The Rowman & Littlefield Publishing Group, Inc.
4501 Forbes Boulevard, Suite 200, Lanham, Maryland 20706
www.rowman.com

86-90 Paul Street, London EC2A 4NE, United Kingdom

British Library Cataloguing in Publication Information Available

Library of Congress Cataloging-in-Publication Data
Names: Jenkins, Sherman L., 1956–
Title: Ted Strong Jr. : the untold story of an original Harlem Globetrotter and
    Negro Leagues All-Star / Sherman L. Jenkins.
Description: Lanham : Rowman & Littlefield, [2016] | Includes bibliographical
    references and index.
Identifiers: LCCN 2016013400 (print) | LCCN 2016024554 (ebook) | ISBN
    9781442267275 (cloth : alk. paper) | ISBN 9781442267282 (electronic) |
    ISBN 9781538192306 (pbk : alk. paper)
Subjects: LCSH: Strong, Jr., Ted, 1917–1978. | Basketball players—United
    States—Biography. | Harlem Globetrotters—History. | Baseball players—
    United States—Biography. | Negro leagues—History.
Classification: LCC GV884.S78 J46 2016 (print) | LCC GV884.S78 (ebook) |
    DDC 796.323092 [B]—dc23
LC record available at https://lccn.loc.gov/2016013400

CONTENTS

PREFACE

Find the good and praise it.

—From the grave marker of Alex Haley in Henning, Tennessee

Englewood High School on the South Side of Chicago on a cold, early November afternoon in 1973: I was a junior looking forward to killing some time before track practice began at five o'clock. I moseyed up to the library on the third floor of the ancient Chicago public school building to review some notes for a pop quiz scheduled in my history class the next day. On my way to the main study room, I met a fellow classmate who was leaving and I noticed to my left a group of guys huddled around a seated student.

I asked my classmate what was going on, and he whispered that Cardell Strong had a book about Negro Leagues baseball and he was showing them that his father and brothers were listed. Cardell and I were neighborhood buddies, and his braggadocio attitude was well known.

Curious, I made my way to the group.

"See, here's my brother, Ted," Cardell said in an excitedly low tone. "I told you," he added as he pointed to the book he had opened on the library table. "You thought I was lying, didn't ya?" he challenged.

As I stepped around the five boys, straining to see what Cardell was pointing to, he spotted me and motioned me to come closer.

"Come here, Sherm. You need to see this, too," he declared. Cardell was an Englewood High School senior, several years older than I. We were from the same Woodlawn neighborhood and knew each other well.

"Man, what are you talking about now?" I said.

"I am showing these guys that my father and brothers played baseball in the old Negro Leagues," he explained.

"What?! Yeah, right," I scoffed.

I moved closer, and Cardell closed the book to show me the title on the cover: *Only the Ball Was White* by Robert Peterson. He reopened it to the page he was showing to the other boys:

STRONG, OTHELLO—1950—p, Chicago American Giants
STRONG, T. R. (TED)—1937–48—of, inf, mgr, Indianapolis Athletics, Indianapolis ABCs, Kansas City Monarchs, Indianapolis Clowns

"See, right here, Strong," he stated and stabbed at the names with his finger. "Ted Strong and Othello Strong are my brothers. My dad played too, but they don't have him in here."

I wondered and thought: What's the Negro Baseball Leagues? It must have been something special to have a book written about it. Well, as I learned much later, the league at one time was an important element in the African American community, and Cardell's brothers and father were part of the league's history. I also discovered what Negro Leagues historians like Robert Peterson showed in his book: Cardell's older brother Ted and their father were often blended as one player because of the closeness of their names. As you read this book, you will see what I mean.

"You see, all you guys thought I was blowing smoke," Cardell exclaimed. "I don't need to make it up. It's right here in black and white. That is why I am such an outstanding athlete."

"Okay, I've heard enough," one of the boys said with a smile.

The bell sounded for the final period of the day.

I realized that I needed to head for track practice. I hadn't noticed how the time had slipped by. Little did I know that this brief episode in my life would revisit me years later in a totally different way.

While taking a summer class in 1977, I was a junior majoring in news/editorial journalism at Northern Illinois University (NIU) in DeKalb. Two weeks into my required Article Writing course, we were given the task of writing a feature story and pitching it to area newspapers to see if we could get it published. I wanted a unique idea for a feature story. As was typical for many NIU students who were from Chicago, I boarded a Greyhound bus and made the sixty-five-mile trek from DeKalb to Woodlawn on Chicago's South Side to spend the weekend at home. I met the fellas and hung out. Cardell Strong and his younger brothers, Bredell and Odell, were with us. I looked at Cardell and immediately knew that I had the subject of my feature article.

"Cardell, remember when you showed us that book with the names of your brothers playing in the old Negro Leagues?" I asked.

"Uh-huh," he replied.

"You think your old man would let me do an article on him?"

"I don't know. You can ask him."

The next day I called Mr. Strong, explained what I was doing, and asked if he would allow me to interview him.

"Surrrre," he replied in his soft, elderly voice.

When I set up our first meeting for the following weekend, I never fathomed that, in addition to the resulting article that I wrote about him for an August 1977 edition of the *Chicago Defender* newspaper, I would also write about his eldest son, Ted Jr. I didn't know about Ted Jr. When Strong Sr. suggested that I write about Ted Jr., I looked at him puzzled, to which Strong Sr. chuckled and explained that Ted Jr. was the oldest child from his first marriage. I knew only of his children like Cardell, Bredell, and others, whose first names ended in "dell," with whom I grew up in the neighborhood. As I conducted my research for this book, the more I learned about the younger son Othello. Strong Sr. mentioned him playing in the Negro Leagues, but not as passionately. I learned that Ode, as Othello was fondly called by childhood friends, learned to play sports from Strong Sr. and briefly became a standout pitcher/player in the Negro Leagues and ManDak Leagues in Canada.

On top of that, who could have known that "life would happen" to me and that thirty-six years later I would write this book about Strong Sr.'s eldest son, who lived an amazing life during the most tumultuous period in African American history?

Before you delve into the story of this unsung hero in Negro sports, let me point out why I wrote this book. First, his full story needed to be told. When I did an Internet search of his name, I got baseball statistics. There wasn't a book written about Ted Jr. He is like the hundreds of African American men and women who played in the Negro Baseball Leagues and are unsung heroes. It is time to use the technology of today to uncover their stories. During my research, I learned about many other authors who have written books on the Negro Leagues. This is encouraging, but more needs to be done. Second, I hope this book provides exposure and clarity and puts to rest long-held misunderstandings about this man. For example, there were two Ted Strongs. The father and oldest son had the same first, middle, and last name: Theodore Relighn Strong. What often didn't make the news stories or documents were the Senior and Junior designations.

Furthermore, there were nicknames that became, over time, blended by Negro Leagues players. You would think that when someone said, "Sure, I remember 'Pops,'" the person would be referring to Ted Strong Sr. And, yes, the person would be correct, but, in the same breath, the person would add that "Pops" played with the Monarchs and the Globetrotters. After producing evidence to the contrary, the person would finally realize, "Oh, I didn't know that. So, that's the father, and the son is the one who played with the Kansas City Monarchs." Similarly, old-timers associated the initials "T. R." to Ted Jr. Those initials had been a long-standing connection to Strong Sr. by close friends, relatives, and Negro Leagues baseball associates. Third, the African American experience that Ted Jr. and his family lived through needs to be told again and again. The 1919 race riots, the Scottsboro Boys, the discrimination against African Americans in the navy during World War II are forgotten until historians bring the experiences to light again so that we never forget the inhumane treatment of fellow human beings.

I grappled briefly with whether to write this book only about Ted Strong Jr. Ted Sr. and others always spoke proudly of Ted Jr., and as I began my research of the *Chicago Defender* archives and other publications, I could only imagine what people witnessed as Ted Jr. played on the baseball diamonds and hardwood courts across this country. To this day I regret the fact that I did not meet Ted Jr. I have wondered if he would have been open to discussing all facets of his life. What were his thoughts about playing with the greats like Satchel Paige, Cool Papa Bell, and Josh Gibson, or on the hardwood floor with Goose Tatum and Marcus Haynes?

One day I asked his youngest sister, Sydell, what Ted Jr. was like around their father Strong Sr.

"Oh, he and the others from Daddy's first marriage were very respectful," she said. "They always said 'yes, sir' and 'no, sir.' And if Daddy would get on him about something, Ted would drop his head and just listen to Daddy. And Ted wasn't a young man then, either."

From that encounter I received my answer. Write the book already. Ted Jr. was the star, the pride and joy of the family and the thousands who witnessed his superb athletic abilities. Yes, his father played an important role in his development, but sports lovers want to know about the exploits of the man who was one of the first two-sports stars of his day. He hit tape-measure home runs, rounded the bases like a locomotive, performed feats of magic with a basketball, and played in some of the most historic sporting events this country has ever known.

When you research the lives of unsung heroes, so many things get uncovered. As Larry Lester, chairman of the Negro Leagues Committee of the Society for American Baseball Research (SABR), states before each annual conference, "We are here to present information. Please don't bash someone because you feel they state something or present material that you feel is incorrect. We are all starving for knowledge, and we all are working together to get it right."

In the spirit of the SABR Negro Leagues Committee, this book is a start at presenting the remarkable story of Ted Strong Jr. to the public. I hope I have done justice to the memory of this African American who did his best to "do the best that he could."

ACKNOWLEDGMENTS

I want to thank so many people and institutions that helped me with this book. If I forget to mention someone, I hope they will find it in their heart to forgive me since this has been a long ordeal.

Let me start the acknowledgments by thanking Mr. Ted Strong Sr. for letting me interview him and for providing me with insights about Ted Jr. Right along with Strong Sr., I want to thank God for keeping the passion alive within me so that I could focus, make this project happen, and keep my promise to Strong Sr. During the years when "life was happening," I always figured that some sportswriter would pen the Ted Strong Jr. story, especially after what I had written in 1978. Unfortunately, no one stepped to the plate. My turn came again, and I decided to swing for the fence. This is my first published book. Whether I have all the pieces in this edition to give you, the reader, an insight into Strong Jr., who made his mark on the African American sports canvas, will remain to be seen. I hope that this book paves the way for more writers, researchers, and historians to delve into his life and other Negro Leagues baseball and basketball heroes and bring their stories to light. It's been decades since the demise of the Negro Baseball Leagues, and we still have only scratched the surface about this American treasure.

Before I leave the Strong family, I must give a great big hug to my childhood friend and daughter of Strong Sr., Sydell Strong Sheehan. She never failed to speak to me and provide whatever she could remember about her father. She is the next to the oldest child from Strong Sr.'s second marriage. (Sydell, you never knew that I had a crush on you when we were in high school, but I figured I was too young for you.) I must also thank Mr. Jasper Strong. When Sydell gave me his contact information and we met, I felt I had a key ally among the children from Strong Sr.'s first marriage. I hoped the oldest living daughter from Strong Sr.'s first marriage, Gwendolyn Strong-Pruett-Hall, would be a conduit to greater insights. She stuck to her guns in not talking with me because "you are talking about my daddy, and you are trying to make money off my daddy." Her nephew, Terry Ellison, explained to me that I shouldn't take it personally because "she told me the same thing." Mr. Ellison desires to learn more about his family and is working to organize a Strong family reunion. Terry, thank you and you know you can count on me. (Gwendolyn Strong-Pruett-Hall passed away July 5, 2015.)

This leads me to another person I want to thank—Mr. Larry Lester, chairman of the Negro Leagues Committee of the Society for American Baseball Research (SABR) and one of the founders of the Negro Leagues Baseball Museum in Kansas City, Missouri. In my opinion, he is one of the premier researchers of Negro Leagues baseball, and I must credit his work with other superb researchers, such as the late Dick Clark and Sammy J. Miller, in the publication of books such as *Black Baseball's National Showcase: The East-West All-Star Game, 1933–1953*; *Black Baseball in Chicago*; and *The Negro Leagues Book*. I contacted him in the early 2000s when I made my first effort to write the book, and he immediately responded to my e-mail and provided some photos of Ted Jr. from his company's collection of photographs of Negro Leagues players. Three years after the first attempt, I reached out to Mr. Lester again, and he graciously provided information. As I have forged ahead with this effort at writing the book, he has responded to every e-mail and telephone call and provided encouragement with the words "Go Strong!" at the end of every e-mail. Larry, you are the best!

My deepest gratitude must go to the men who knew Ted Jr. and/or Othello. Many of those people who knew Ted Jr. and Othello have gone on to be with the Lord, but the ones who I had the fortune to meet and interview like Alvin Spearman, Rev. Morris Gordon, and Timuel D. Black Jr., were most gracious with their time and insight. My God, I hope that if I reach their age my memory is as sharp. Oral historians such as these men are rare.

I want to thank East Aurora High School; the Aurora Public Library; the Chicago Public Schools (especially William Gerstein, Barry Shore, Marcus Thomas); the Chicago Public Library and its Vivian G. Harsh Research Collection staff (especially Ms. Beverly A. Cook); St. Joseph County Public Library in South Bend, Indiana; Mystery Street Recording Company in Chicago for transferring the audio interview of Ted Strong Sr. from reel-to-reel to digital CD; Terri Winston of the *Chicago Defender*,

Vicki Wilson of Johnson Publishing Company, LLC; and authors John Christgau, Donald Spivey, Jo Fredell Higgins, Robert Renteria Jr., Phil Dixon, and Ryan Whirty. I must give a big hug to fellow Englewood High School alum Vincent Price, who is the son of Bernie Price, the longtime friend and Globetrotter teammate of Ted Jr. He shared various articles, stories, and pictures that he had in his possession regarding his famous father.

I must thank my editors starting with Ms. Jill Wold, who painstakingly read my first draft of the manuscript and provided comments and criticisms that guided me in the right direction to make this book possible. The following men and women offered help and encouragement to stay the course: Sharon Morrow, Judy Dawson, Ron Ford, Tony Hylton, Mike Rogers, Robert Renteria Jr., Emily Johnson and Richard Gilreath (reference interns at the Dolph Briscoe Center for American History in Austin, Texas), Maria De Leon (U.S. congressman Bill Foster's office), Beverly A. Cook, Katie Way of the St. Joseph County Health Department, my goddaughter Cassandra Hayden, my daughter-in-law Tiffany Munnerlyn, Lt. Jermaine J. Jemmott, Illinois state representative Stephanie Kifowit, Emily Ferguson, Kathy Leonard, James and Wanda Bass, Mr. and Mrs. Edward Cox, Floyd Garrett, Kidada Robinson of Aurora University, Greg Backes, Harriet Parker of Waubonsee Community College, Ron Allen for providing valuable insights into getting a book published since he had just published his own, author Cheryl Gist-Williams who also shared valuable insights, poet Karen Fullett-Christensen, Leslie Heaphy of the SABR Negro Leagues Committee, Patricia Arnold, Walter Leavy, Sheree Franklin, Crystal L. Gross, sister-in-law Terrie Outley, Aurora Noon Rotary members who always asked about the status of the book, Sally Rutledge-Ott, Kristi Gliksman Turchi, Dee Massey, Alison D. Hillen of Morgan State University, Fran Judkins of the Naismith Memorial Basketball Hall of Fame, Dr. Jeremy Krock of the SABR Negro Leagues Committee, Brett Meister, Harlem Globetrotters International, Inc., Patricia Andrews Keenan, and Walter Leavy.

Another round of thanks goes to Rowman & Littlefield for recognizing the importance of Ted Jr.'s story and the company's willingness to publish it. Acquisitions Editor Christen Karniski stayed with me as I pitched the Ted Jr. book idea to her verbally at the national Society for American Baseball Research (SABR) convention in Chicago in 2015 and finally with a written book proposal. In my biased opinion, Rowman & Littlefield is another publisher that is willing to step forward and publish the vast works about Negro Leagues baseball.

Last but not least my wife, Juliette; my children, Ayanna, Kwasi, and my stepson Ondrea; my grandson Jai, who accompanied me on many library visits; my granddaughter Makala; and my cousin Jerry Bemley. I know this book project was something many of you couldn't understand. I lost count of how many times I heard, "Why are you doing this?" This was the book within me, and I thank God for allowing all of you to bear with me as I completed this journey. I made a promise to Strong Sr. I feel my life would not be complete if I didn't keep my promise.

1

IT STARTED WITH A SENIOR

On an extremely hot and muggy Sunday afternoon on the South Side of Chicago in 1977, a group of youngsters agreed to unload 4,200 watermelons off a semitruck and stack them in a warehouse. At a steady pace, they unloaded the watermelons into large cardboard boxes.

After about an hour, they began to slow their pace. When one of the overseers of the operation yelled, "Break time," the teenagers slumped down in their places and sighed with relief.

Five minutes later, they noticed a fragile, gray-haired old man approach them pointing in the direction of the watermelons on the truck. "C'mon, you youngsters, let's get back to work." The youngsters obeyed because they knew this man.

He was eighty-three-year-old Rev. Theodore Strong Sr., literate theologian and president of the Pathfinders, a community organization that had purchased the watermelons to provide jobs for young African Americans out of work. The Pathfinders taught religion, economics, and metaphysics, and at one point in the seventies there were approximately three thousand members in the organization, according to William Gipson, who served as Pathfinder director at the time.

Strong Sr., after sleeping only five hours and eating once, tried to help unload the truck, but the workers drove him away. "No, you go back to the car and rest. You've done enough for today." After a little resistance, he slowly made his way back to the car. "I'm going home now, but if you need anything, call me," he said.

Some Pathfinder members expressed concern and admiration for the reverend. "He always has a way of getting things done. But Mr. Strong should let us young people take care of lifting and pushing of these watermelons while he rests," Gipson said. Cardell Strong, Pathfinder secretary

1

and son of Strong Sr., said, "He works so hard to achieve so much for his community. He sat up most of the night waiting for the call from the truck driver who brought the watermelons in from the South. He knows his doctor would get angry if he found out about that, but Dad says there is too much work to be done and he can't rest."

After being driven by one of his sons, Strong Sr. was back home relaxing but just as eager to return to the warehouse. "They think I've done too much, but I can handle it," he insisted. "I'm really glad that truck came in today. Now we can provide some income for the young people in the community."

Strong Sr. and the Pathfinders purchased the warehouse the watermelons were being stored in earlier that year. Strong Sr. negotiated with the Department of Urban Renewal in Chicago to rehabilitate various homes on the South Side that had been abandoned by landlords.

"We try to rehabilitate the properties in order to provide a chance in life for some needy person," Strong Sr. said.

Strong Sr. had been active in the black community on the South Side most of his life, and his history illuminates the African American experience.

On June 3, 1894, he became the fifth of eleven children born to Osborne and Angeline Talley Strong in Little Rock, Arkansas. Eighteen years earlier, Osborne and Angeline were married by Judge Nelson J. Kelley on December 27. To have their marriage recorded, showing that this partnership occurred, was important because Angeline was white and Osborne was a light-skinned Negro who probably passed for white.

This union provided brothers and sisters for little Ted Strong Sr., whom he would come to admire and depend upon. The oldest sibling, Samuel, was a laborer in the local railroad shop by the age of twenty-two. Sometime prior to Samuel's employment in the railroad shop, his mother Angeline became ill and died. To make matters worse, Strong Sr.'s second-oldest brother, Jasper, who didn't have much love for white people, ventured into a saloon, began pestering some of the white patrons, and was killed when one of the patrons pulled a gun and shot him in the head.

After this incident, coming on the heels of losing their mother, Strong Sr. and the other older brothers and sisters focused on handling the chores and responsibilities assigned to them by their father, who now had to raise them alone.

Little Strong Sr. was six years old when his mother died. His father managed to hold the family together until he became ill and died at the age of fifty-four in 1904, leaving the children to relatives. An adventurous and determined streak had already developed in Strong Sr. He felt that he would be better off with his brother who had left Arkansas a few months earlier. He learned that his brother had traveled to Chicago, and he was going to leave to join him, if he could find him. So for about six weeks at the age of ten, he got the idea to join a circus in order to earn enough money to travel to Chicago.

After working various jobs in the local circus, he earned the money he needed to reach Chicago, and during the latter part of 1904, Strong Sr. finally made his way to the Windy City. But fate would not allow him to find his brother so easily, as Strong Sr. learned that his brother had moved to Aurora, Illinois, a blue-collar town forty miles west of Chicago. In 1900, the city of Aurora had a population of 24,147. Most of the people in Aurora at that time migrated there to find work in the industrial town that was quickly developing.[1]

As historian Dennis Buck points out in his book *From Slavery to Glory: African Americans Come To Aurora, Illinois 1850–1920*:

> Aurora followed a path similar to Chicago, her mammoth neighbor to the east. The rail lines that connected the two cities benefited Aurora economically. However, she was not overwhelmed and absorbed by Chicago. Partly, this was due to distance, Aurora being around 40 miles to the west. More importantly, Aurora developed and maintained a distinct identity. The addition of fast and reliable transportation to the existing mix of industry and trade made Aurora a logical place for new industries to locate. A diverse range of business and manufacturing, from casting and assembling iron cooking stoves to sewing ladies underwear, settled into the area to take advantage of the vast markets made possible by the Chicago, Burlington and Quincy Railroad (C.B.&O). Each new venture meant jobs. Immigrants from Sweden, Germany, Ireland, Romania and Luxembourg, as well as migrants from states in the South and East, followed the siren call of economic opportunity to Aurora. By 1870, this included a growing enclave of African Americans.[2]

After a few hours in Chicago, Strong, Sr. was given directions to Aurora. He paid his twenty-five-cent one-way fare and boarded either the Chicago Aurora and Elgin Railroad or the Chicago, Burlington and Quincy Railroad for the seventy-five-minute ride to Aurora, where after several hours he found his brother. This ten-year-old was determined. Among the things that probably made it easier for Strong Sr. to find Samuel is that around the time he arrived in Aurora, the African American population hovered near the three hundred mark. As with other nationalities, African Americans congregated among themselves. Therefore, asking African Americans about his brother would eventually produce the answer he desired. His brother lived on Aurora's East Side at 421 Watson, and Strong Sr. joined him and quickly took measures to not be a burden to his brother and future wife, Celica Ann Harding.

"I took on various jobs as a laborer," Strong Sr. said. This was not uncommon, and again historian Dennis Buck points out:

> One such issue is whether to interpret adulthood as a chronological age or as a cultural category based on independence, abilities and responsibilities? The censuses reveal numerous examples of African American children as young as thirteen employed full-time and part-time, and living independently as boarders or in the home of their employers. Postslavery African American culture may have considered teenagers adults, or poverty may have pushed children to take on extra obligations.[3]

Strong Sr. lived with his brother while attending grammar school. When Strong Sr. entered East Aurora High School sometime around 1907, he became interested in sports. For a couple of years, he worked as a waiter in a cafeteria so he could continue his education.

In April of 1908, Samuel Lee Strong married Celica Ann Harding. Strong Sr.'s brother worked most of the time, so he helped around the house. "My brother's wife treated me as though I was her own child," Strong said. "She helped me acquire my education."[4]

Strong's sense of independence saw him move out of his brother's home, and he became a boarder at Indiana Avenue between Kane and Pond Avenue.[5] Shortly after Strong Sr. left, Samuel took in his baby sister Bessie, who was twelve years old. In 1919 Bessie Strong graduated from East Aurora High School.

Per interviews with Strong Sr., he stated that he graduated from East Aurora in 1911. However, searches of available records and documents from East Aurora High School and the Aurora Public Library did not uncover confirmation of Strong Sr.'s graduation from the school. It appears that the lure of "big city" Chicago saw Strong Sr. making trips there before graduating. He spent some time at Chicago's Moody Bible Institute, where it was noted that he accepted Christ. Historical records indicate that he attended high school, lived in Chicago, and did mission work.[6]

Apparently, Strong Sr. left Aurora for Chicago to seek a way of life for himself. Strong said that he found work as a dishwasher in a restaurant for seventy-five cents a day. This helped him to pay his rent and obtain meals. But longing for something more than just washing dishes, Strong Sr.'s interest soon turned to the medical field.

After a short experience in medical school, he quit and decided he wanted to be a boxer. "It [medical school] became so difficult and so tough on me. I decided this was not the life for me. I wanted to be a boxer so I could make some quick money," Strong Sr. said.[7]

Strong Sr. made some quick money. Within a span of four years, he won sixty-nine fights and lost none as a lightweight. In 1915, Strong Sr. fought his last fight against a lightweight fighter by the name of Kid Henry. Although he defeated Henry in three rounds, Strong admitted it wasn't easy.

"I took a good licking from Kid Henry," Strong Sr. said, looking down and shaking his head slowly. "He knocked me down in the first round, but I got up and beat him."[8]

During his boxing career, he played baseball in the summer months and was considered a pretty good prospect. This led Strong Sr. into the Negro Leagues as a pitcher with the American Giants. Strong Sr. is listed on the 1913 Chicago American Giants roster as a pitcher.[9] He played with legendary players such as Andrew "Rube" Foster, known as the father of Negro Leagues baseball.

Sometime around 1916, while playing semi-pro baseball, the twenty-two-year-old Strong Sr. spent time in South Bend, Indiana. In the 1916 city directory, he is listed working as a porter and rooming at 418 S. Main Street. South Bend had become a hub for industrial activity as companies such as Singer, Studebaker, and Westinghouse located there, and the city became a magnet drawing people to the opportunities of jobs and a better way of life. Young Ted Strong Sr. was one of those people who took on odd jobs to make a living. Around this time, the African American population in South Bend was heavily concentrated on the city's West Side. As with other American cities experiencing population growth, South Bend was no different. Its population increased by 35 percent between 1910 and 1920. However, with plentiful jobs came conflict as white immigrants and African Americans from the South competed for housing and jobs.

The athletic-minded Strong Sr. just wanted to make a living and play sports. The racial divide occurred in housing, public accommodations, and other areas of life in South Bend including sports. While South Bend's entry into professional baseball is recorded to be around 1903 as a member of the Central League, years later African Americans had to develop their own baseball league teams. In the summer of 1916, Strong Sr. played for and managed the South Bend Colored Giants.

During the summer of 1916, the olive-skinned, lanky young man met eighteen-year-old Vera Leona Smith, who was attending school. She was born May 1, 1898, in Chattanooga, Tennessee. She was the second-oldest of five children born to Alonzo and Rosa Smith. After a short courtship, Strong Sr. and Vera were married on October 30, 1916. They started their family early, as three months later on January 2, 1917, they became the proud parents of their first child, Ted Strong Jr. As the years progressed, thirteen more children followed and Strong Sr. continued to play baseball and work odd jobs. He continued to pitch with the Giants until a salary dispute caused him to leave. He journeyed back and forth into baseball with different teams because "I loved the game so much," Strong Sr. said.[10]

In June of 1917, Strong Sr. and Vera moved to an apartment at 4816 S. Langley in Chicago to settle and raise a family, though one child died after falling from a porch and three others were stillborn.

The Strongs constantly worked to better life for their family. They were among the thousands of African Americans migrating to Chicago. Between 1910 and 1920, fifty thousand African Americans streamed to Chicago's Black Belt. The population in the Black Belt tripled, rising from 34,335 to 92,501, which constituted the bulk of Chicago's African American population. Despite the overcrowded conditions and few job opportunities, Strong Sr., at the age of twenty-seven, managed to secure employment as a butcher at Morris & Co at the Union Stock Yards in Chicago.

"He always had something going," said Jasper Strong.[11] Even though Jasper was not born until 1939, he related what he heard from his older brothers and sisters and what he eventually experienced as a young boy growing up in a large household.

"I remember my father taking me to boxing matches. I remember seeing Sugar Ray Robinson versus Carmen Basilio," Jasper said. "My mother worked all the time. She did domestic work while my dad worked as a painter."[12]

Jasper fondly remembers going on picnics in nearby Washington Park with the family. "My father would cook and my mother would prepare a basket and we would walk to the park and just have a grand time," Jasper said smiling. "My father always had us involved in some kind of sports. I remember as a 'shorty' he was teaching me how to box. My father would take us to the 51st Street gym and my brother Ted would spar with Joe Louis."

"Joe Louis broke my brother's nose," Jasper said.[13] Strong Sr. said that Ted was "big" for his age, and he always wanted to have his children involved in some activity to keep them from getting in trouble. Strong

Sr.'s community involvement had him on the go constantly. His efforts to improve the lives of his family and fellow African Americans drew him into a period of strife that scarred the lives of all Chicagoans: the 1919 race riots. At the time of the July 1919 riots, Strong Sr. and his family were renting an apartment at 5263 S. Dearborn Street.

The Strong family was probably trying to beat the ninety-degree temperatures on that fateful July 27 day when five African American boys ventured to a "private spot" they knew between the black-patronized 25th Street beach and the "white" beach at 29th Street behind Michael Reese Hospital. The boys had a raft they built that unfortunately drifted into an area where "the fury of racial hatred had just erupted."[14]

Defying the unwritten law, which designated that beach as exclusively white, several black men and women had strolled to 29th Street determined to enter the water. Curses, threatening gestures, and rocks frightened the interlopers away. Minutes later, however, their numbers reinforced, the blacks reappeared, this time hurling rocks. The white bathers fled. But the blacks' possession of the beach was only temporary; behind a barrage of stones white bathers and numerous sympathizers returned. The battle that ensued was frightening in its violence, but it merely anticipated Chicago's long-feared race war. Innocently unaware of the savage exchange of projectiles and angry words at 29th Street, the five boys continued to "swim, kick, dive, and play around." One of the five boys, seventeen-year-old Eugene Williams, was hit by a projectile and drowned. This now-famous incident ignited the 1919 race riot. "The rioting raged virtually uncontrolled for the greater part of five days. Day and night white toughs assaulted isolated blacks, and teenage black mobsters beat white peddlers and merchants in the black belt. . . . White gunmen in automobiles sped through the black belt shooting indiscriminately as they passed, and black snipers fired back."[15]

One evening during the five-day rampage, Strong Sr. was heading home from a community meeting. He heard a car gunning its engine and coming in his direction.

"I remember hearing my brothers asking my dad about the 1919 riots. He told them that it was a bad time and one night he barely escaped with his life," Jasper related. "When he heard the car screeching and moving in his direction, he heard gun shots. My dad got behind a telephone pole just in time. He said had he not jumped behind that pole, he would have been killed and I never would be here talking to you."[16]

Life still went on during this five-day period, and Strong Sr. went to work. On August 2, 1919, he is seen among other African American South

Side residents in a photograph taken by a photographer assigned to cover the event for a local news organization. In 1980 while visiting Strong Sr. at his home, I was reading a Sunday, February 3, 1980, edition of the *Chicago Tribune*. Veteran African American newspaper columnist Vernon Jarrett penned a Black History Month perspective feature titled "Remembering Black Chicago." The article reflected on the life and times of various African American Chicago residents and spotlighted the trials and successes of lawyer Earl B. Dickerson, musician Theodore "Red" Saunders, and journalist Lovelyn Evans. A portion of the article included the photograph taken August 2, 1919. Strong Sr. asked me what I was reading. I showed him the newspaper and specifically the photograph at the same time, asking him if he remembered the 1919 riots.

"Yep, I do," he replied matter-of-factly. Pointing at the photograph, he said, "That's me there."

I sat stunned. The tall, slim, handsome guy turning to his left as he strolled across the street in a white shirt and derby hat was Strong Sr. He was on his way to work and noticed out of the corner of his eye a man with a camera. The picture became one of hundreds taken by local and national photographers covering the worst race riot in American history.

Life happened again, and we didn't get to discuss that event in his life in more detail. I can only imagine what it was like trying to be a human being, raise a family, work for a living if possible, and attempt to enjoy life in a city crowded with others trying to do the same thing. To have an incident of the magnitude of the race riot—where another race of people kills a child of your own race, who was trying to cool off, and you must contend with thugs driving through your community shooting at other members of your race because they could—just shows how vulnerable African Americans were. However, the courage and determination of Strong Sr. just confirmed the superior resiliency of African Americans when you consider the aftermath of the riot.

As outlined in the book, *The Politics of Riot Commissions* by Anthony M. Platt, one of the unfortunate aftermaths of the 1919 riot was the number of injuries that occurred in the Black Belt. Overall, 38 persons were killed, 537 injured, and more than 1,000 left homeless.

In many American history books, the 1920s were the "Roaring Twenties." America was emerging from World War I and the industrial age began in earnest. For most African Americans in Chicago's Black Belt, however, just surviving was an accomplishment. Strong Sr. had another mouth to feed in 1922 when daughter Vera came into the world. But his desire to see his "race" advance tugged at him even more. Shortly after the birth of Vera, he and several members of his neighborhood launched the Afro National Economic League, a community-based economic development organization. The group began by approaching one of the most profitable entities in the African American community at that time, the Roosevelt-Bankers State Bank, and with financing provided by the bank acquired residential properties to rehabilitate and then lease to African Americans who were coming to Chicago from the South.

"Roosevelt Bank was located at that time at 31st and State Street. The bank also turned over to us the old Epiphany Temple and Royal Gardens located at the 400 block east on 31st Street," Strong Sr. said.[17] "We operated [Royal Gardens] for two years so that we could rehabilitate it and use it for a center for the youth. It was a beautiful structure built in the late 1890s for that purpose."[18]

Unfortunately, the Afro National Economic League eventually lost the properties through "negligence and discontentment," Strong Sr. said. "Blacks who had a little money wanted to run it for other purposes. Politicians, who depended upon pimps, prostitution and gambling to be elected, they fought me pretty hard," he said.[19]

Strong Sr. sought the advice of many African Americans who could counsel him on "the ways of blacks in Chicago." "Ed Wright was the best black leader black people had," according to Strong Sr. "He did more to enlighten me to the ways of blacks in Chicago."[20] Edward Herbert Wright was the first African American committeeman in the Second Ward of Chicago. Wright was in his late fifties at the time Strong Sr. met him in the 1920s, when he and other African American politicians took control of the predominantly black Second Ward, initiating the development of the nation's most powerful black political organization. Wright told Strong Sr. that the NAACP and the Urban League could only do so much to help blacks in Chicago.

"The white [power] structure used the NAACP and other groups and kept them going," Strong Sr. lamented. "Ed Wright showed me a lot."[21]

Strong Sr. knew hard work and determination would help him and his Afro National Economic League organization succeed. Strong Sr. wasn't a quitter. He kept the organization going until 1948, trying to improve the conditions for African Americans on the South Side.

While he was an active member of his community, Strong Sr. continued to make time for his children. His eldest son, Ted Jr., by 1925, was eight years old and was beginning to show an interest in sports. Strong Sr. began to take Ted Jr. with him to the gym when he sparred for boxing and to practice fields where Negro Leagues baseball players trained during the baseball season. Strong Sr. didn't want his son involved in the dangerous behavior that he witnessed among some of the neighborhood kids.

"I would walk down the street and I'd see youth at an early age rob a bakery truck or steal meat off a meat truck. My heart went out because I knew that this was a plight that couldn't exist and be fruitful," he lamented. "So I wanted to put together an athletic program that would interest the youth. Being athletically inclined myself, being of a clear mind, I thought that we should have good healthy bodies," Strong Sr. added.[22]

He tried to get professionals such as doctors and lawyers in the community to be sponsors of the athletic program, but he found few takers, forcing him to give up on the idea until a change of venue rekindled it.

"We moved from the far South Side at 5263 Dearborn to 4233 Wabash, where I became interested in the youth there," he recalled.[23]

2

"TED WAS BIG FOR HIS AGE"

Strong Sr. organized a group of youth to play basketball. "Iron Man" McGinnis, Bernie Price, Inman Jackson, Hillard Brown, to name a few, were members of a basketball group called the Black Panthers. Strong Sr. and several of his friends took the youths to various vacant lots to play basketball against other youths from other neighborhoods in the Black Belt. Strong Sr. and his friends showed the boys how to perfect their basketball skills. The boys worked hard and responded well to the attention they received from Strong Sr. and others in the neighborhood. Strong Sr. said the youths were good, and he again approached various professionals in the community for sponsorship.

In late 1927 at 47th and South Parkway (now Dr. Martin Luther King Jr. Drive), developers constructed the Savoy Ballroom. Strong Sr. and his friends thought it would be good to call the basketball group the Savoy Big Five. They approached the Savoy Ballroom management and obtained a promise that the boys would receive shirts with Savoy Big Five written on them. The youths played for a while under the name Savoy Big Five, but the boys never got their shirts, so Strong Sr. and friends decided to change the name back to the Black Panthers. There is a possibility that the reason the boys didn't get the shirts stemmed from what was being developed by the ownership of the Savoy. The sports landscape in the 1920s in a big city like Chicago was vast. Groups like the one Strong Sr. had organized were everywhere. Playing different teams from various neighborhoods created rivalries that became legend, and venues like the Savoy wanted a piece of the action. Talented basketball and baseball players abounded. When the Savoy Ballroom was built, it included a department store, and eventually the Regal Theatre. The Savoy was the scene of huge dance crowds as the "big band" era blossomed during the Roaring Twenties. When no bands were scheduled, the owners needed something to fill the void. One of the owners, Dick Hudson, brought in a local team called the Giles Post American Legion Quintet as an experiment. He hired a young man named Abe Saperstein as his coach. "Although only 5'3½" tall, Abe had won fifteen letters at Lake View High School in Chicago and had been a star backcourt man on the basketball team. After graduation, he played for the Chicago Reds from 1920 to '25. He turned from playing to coaching and promoting games in 1926."[1]

This experiment became popular. After financial and contractual difficulties between Hudson and his business partners developed, Saperstein formed a team: "Saperstein took some of the players, added some other local talent and booked a game in Hinckley, Illinois, fifty miles southwest of Chicago, for the night of January 7, 1927. This was the first game for a team called 'Saperstein's New York,' a name chosen to imply the team was not local."[2] It was important to make the distinction because throughout the United States local baseball, basketball, and football teams were prevalent. Many of the teams were products of businesses that wanted to give their employees a recreational release from work and get publicity at the same time. Moreover, local church, civic, and community groups formed teams, and often rivalries and neighborhood reputations developed that lasted for decades.

When the Savoy Ballroom sponsorship didn't materialize, Strong Sr. said that a parent of one of the youths in the Black Panther group contacted Abe Saperstein. The timing was coincidental but history saw fit to link the two disputes—Strong Sr.'s and the shirts and Dick Hudson's with the Savoy management—to allow a basketball troupe idea to develop. Some of the players that Strong Sr. worked with were probably known to Saperstein, but here was a group of youths organized by adults who were offering what he wanted to do—coach and promote.

"Saperstein, at that time, was a big name in Negro sports," Strong Sr. said. "We wanted to take the boys to other cities to play different teams, but we didn't have the money. We knew the boys were good. I later decided to turn the operation over to Saperstein because he had the necessary capital."[3]

In 1929, Ted Strong Jr. entered Wendell Phillips High School and got involved with other neighborhood youths in basketball and baseball. "Ted was big for his age," Strong Sr. said. "He was sports-minded."[4]

Ted Jr. had a great sports foundation. His father and his neighborhood friends helped him to develop skills that attracted the attention of many. Saperstein was one of them. He saw a good thing in the touring basketball team that was dropped in his lap, and he knew he needed superb players like Ted Strong Jr. The Saperstein New York team just played basketball games in the area, and when time permitted he would visit Strong Sr. to get permission to have Ted Jr. join his team after he graduated from Wendell Phillips High School.

While Strong Sr. continued his involvement with the Negro Baseball Leagues and remained a community activist, he had to work with his wife to run a household that now contained five additional children besides Ted Jr.: Nathaniel, Ollie, Othello, Charlotte, and Gwendolyn. As with many African American families in Chicago at that time, the Strong family helped family members whenever they could. The 1930 Census shows that Vera's mother, Rosa Smith, age fifty-five, was a part of the household in addition to a "lodger" by the name of Jessie Roland. Lodgers were commonplace whether you had the space or not in order to bring in additional revenue to help pay the rent. However, more to the point, the African American population continued to expand as the lure of jobs and a better way of life attracted men, women, and children to Chicago's Black Belt.

As African Americans continued to flock to Chicago, they, like other nationalities, tried to find ways to have fun and seek entertainment. One of the biggest attractions involved the Century of Progress World's Fair of 1933 and 1934. Strong Sr. said he made sure that he took his children, who now had expanded to seven, to "expose them to things."[5] The fair opened May 28, 1933, and was looked upon as an economic stimulus to jolt Chicago back to the prosperity of the 1920s. Nearly twenty-eight million people went through its turnstiles. As African Americans went to the fair to see what the talk was about, they had to fight for jobs during a time when the national economy compounded the frustrations already experienced in an overpopulated Black Belt.[6] According to noted author and businessman Dempsey Travis in his book *The Autobiography of Black Chicago*:

> The World's Fair of 1933 found the Chicago Urban League with a full-time staff of one. That was the Executive Secretary, A. L. Foster, who tried to get both white collar and menial jobs for the Blacks at the World's Fair. But the placement of menial jobs was given to a white employment agency. According to Willie Randall, the orchestra leader, the only black professionals working on the fair grounds were musicians, members of the Freddie Williams Orchestra, playing at the Jensen Pavilion.[7]

The World's Fair served as a temporary relief valve after African Americans and the world had to contend with the horrendous case of the Scottsboro

Boys. In Alabama in 1931, nine African American teenagers were accused of raping two white women. The case against the nine was first heard in Scottsboro, in three separate trials where the teenagers received poor legal representation. Eight of the nine teenagers were convicted of rape and sentenced to death. The youngest teen, thirteen-year-old Eugene Williams, was granted a new trial by the Alabama Supreme Court because he was a juvenile. The African American community was outraged and protested the case vigorously throughout the country. On May 8, 1933, four thousand African American and white citizens marched more than six miles through a steady rain in Washington, D.C., demanding freedom for the Scottsboro Boys and other prisoners. The May 10, 1933, edition of the *New York Amsterdam News* reported:

> With the 3,000 Negro protesters there were approximately 1,000 white workers who added their voices to the demand for the release of the Scottsboro boys. Among these was Ruby Bates, defense witness in the celebrated case, and she with Mrs. Jamie Patterson, mother of one of the condemned boys, led the parade through the rain-soaked streets of Washington.[8]

As this and other trials and tribulations occurred throughout the nation and Chicago's Black Belt, Strong Sr. and his wife did what they could to provide for their children. Mrs. Strong worked as a domestic, and her husband continued to participate in various capacities in the Negro Baseball Leagues and performed odd jobs when he could. Their children were growing, with the oldest already in high school. Who could predict what life had in store for the family? One certainty emerged: Strong Sr.'s sports tutelage of Ted Jr. would soon pay dividends that would last a long time.

3

TED JR. COMES INTO HIS OWN

Shortly after Ted Jr. entered Wendell Phillips, his muscular six-foot-two-inch frame made him stand out among his peers. People who knew him spoke about his fun-loving and easygoing personality. He immediately gravitated to sports since he knew a number of the guys on the basketball and baseball teams that were tops in Chicago high school sports.

When he wasn't in school Ted Jr. could be found on a sandlot or makeshift basketball court competing against some of the best talent the Black Belt produced at that time. This focus on sports improved his skills tremendously, but schoolwork suffered. He completed courses at Wendell Phillips High School in February 1936.

It wasn't long before Saperstein was back at Strong's home. Strong Sr. finally agreed to let Ted Jr. join Saperstein's team when Saperstein promised he would send Ted Jr. to Morehouse College in Atlanta, Georgia. But Saperstein never sent Ted Jr. to Morehouse; instead, seventeen-year-old Ted Jr. would play center and guard during basketball season later that year with a team that would make history.

While one sports love received satisfaction, the primary sport still lay in wait for Ted Jr. His baseball skills were exceptional, and Strong Sr. worked with his contacts at the Chicago American Giants to get Ted Jr. a tryout. At the start of the season in 1936, Ted Jr. began his baseball career as a shortstop with the Giants. His exposure to the world of Negro Leagues baseball through his father and the "street training" he experienced with the older boys in the neighborhood helped him to mature as an athlete well beyond his years. Confident in his abilities and probably joking around, Ted Jr. and Eddie Brown of the American Giants made a wager with a local Chicago sportswriter that "they would hit over 15 home runs"[1] during the 1936 season. Ted Jr. didn't win the bet, but his participation with the baseball team prepared him physically for the start of the 1936–1937 basketball season with the Harlem Globetrotters.

Somewhere between the summer of 1936 and the winter of 1937, it was reported that Ted Jr. attended Morgan College in Baltimore, Maryland. (Morgan College is now known as Morgan State University, a predominately African American university.) Although his attendance is unconfirmed, he was part of the bill advertising the appearance of the Harlem Globetrotters in Helena, Montana, to face the local college's hoop team. An article in the February 15, 1937, edition of the *Helena Daily Independent* indicated that Ted Jr. was "a new guard, starred at Morgan College in Baltimore and last summer was a sensation at shortstop for the Chicago American Giants baseball team. He owns the largest pair of hands in basketball." A youthful Ted Jr. is pictured palming a basketball with Globetrotters Inman Jackson, Bob Frazier, Bill Ford, Johnny Watts, and Harry Rusan.

The idea that Ted Jr. attended Morgan College seems to have some validity. Abe Saperstein had agreed to send the young budding star to Morehouse College as Strong Sr. asked; however, Ted Jr. did not graduate from Wendell Phillips. No records were located indicating his graduation. What can be surmised is that Abe Saperstein couldn't pull enough strings to get Ted Jr. into the prestigious Morehouse, especially since Ted Jr. didn't have a degree, but small, northeastern Morgan College would suffice.

As Ted Jr. completed his first basketball season with the Globetrotters, Strong Sr. continued his activities with baseball. He obtained the coaching job with the Indianapolis Athletics for the 1937 campaign. On a chilly spring day in May 1937, the ball club entertained three hundred fans who braved the weather to watch the team conduct a practice game with Indiana's best semi-pro team, the Indianapolis Baby Lincolns. Ted Jr. was there for the practice game, and he helped the Athletics to a 5–1 victory with a homer in the fifth inning with two men on base. An article in the *Chicago Defender* reported that Strong Sr. served as manager of the team. The prospects for the upcoming season were great for the team, but to make the season a resounding success, Strong Sr. touted that he would bring his son to the squad. Strong Sr. went out on a limb since he would need to purchase Ted Jr.'s services from the Chicago American Giants and not interfere with junior's Globetrotter job.

Ted Jr.'s stock rose as he burst onto the scene with the Chicago American Giants in 1936 as a shortstop and then teamed up with his father in Indianapolis. Ted Jr.'s stellar performance with the Harlem Globetrotters, combined with his baseball prowess, propelled him to rising star status during the hard economic times of the 1930s.

A number of circumstances allowed Ted Jr.'s star to shine brightly but also to be overshadowed by other well-known African Americans such as Leroy "Satchel" Paige and heavyweight boxing champion Joe Louis. Paige's reputation as one of baseball's best pitchers had become international with him receiving $30,000 for pitching in the Dominican Republic.[2]

The other circumstance that garnered the attention and celebration of African Americans in Chicago's Black Belt was the capturing of the world's heavyweight boxing championship belt by Joe Louis when, on June 22, 1937, the Brown Bomber decked James J. Braddock in the eighth round. The late Chicago African American real estate mogul and noted historian Dempsey Travis wrote:

> When Joe Louis knocked James Braddock d.o.a. (dead on his ass) in the eighth round, my head reeled. . . . I did not have to wonder what the black community thought because the South Side had gone totally berserk, with black people running up and down streets shouting, crying, laughing, and singing as if the millennium had come.[3]

With two of Black America's sources of pride garnering the headlines and dominating the talk of local barber and beauty shops, Ted Jr.'s stock rose with little fanfare until he was selected to black America's premier sporting event: the Negro Leagues East-West All-Star Game, which had started in 1933. It was an All-Star game and World Series rolled into one. In those days, baseball fans who voted through Black America's two largest newspapers, the *Chicago Defender* and the *Pittsburgh Courier*, chose members of the East and West squads. Ted Jr. received 50,636 votes to represent the Indianapolis Athletics as the first baseman/shortstop, the largest vote total for any of the players in the 1937 spectacle. The stage was set, and Ted Strong Jr. made everyone proud.

On August 8, 1937, the sun shone brightly in Chicago as the fifth annual Negro Baseball League East-West All-Star Game got under way in Comiskey Park before twenty thousand fans. Ted Jr. joined some of the best performers of the Negro National and American leagues. Two of the players in the game would decades later be named to Baseball's Hall of Fame: pitcher Hilton Smith and outfielder Turkey Stearnes. Rounding out some of the outstanding talent on the 1937 All-Star squad were pitcher Ted Trent; catchers Double Duty Radcliffe and Frank Duncan;

second basemen Newt Allen and Sammy T. Hughes; and outfielders Willard Brown and Jimmie Crutchfield.

The All-Star series was tied at two wins apiece, and the pitching of the West would have to offset a second consecutive win by the East. The West sent Ted Treat of the American Giants to the mound with the East countering with Slim Jones of the Philadelphia Eagles, both veterans of All-Star competition. The sluggers of the East started their bombardment of the West in the second inning with Buck Leonard, the husky first baseman, sending a home run into the upper deck of the right field seats at Comiskey Park.

The East got a couple of more runs to lead 3–0 going into the fourth inning. Nevertheless, the West got untracked with Ted Jr. driving in a run with a single in the sixth. With the West trailing 3–1, Ted Jr. batted in the sixth with nobody on. Ted Jr. used his six-foot-six-inch, 180-pound frame to slap a drive to the center field wall. A *Chicago Defender* newspaper columnist reported, "When the ball bounced back into the outfield, Strong rounded third like a big locomotive being waved on home by Candy Jim Taylor."[4] Ted Jr. used his speed and what was reported as a mishandling of the ball by the outfielder to score an inside-the-park home run.

While several errors by Ted Jr. and other West players helped the East to a 7–2 win, Ted Jr. made a good showing in his first All-Star contest. Another article in the *Defender* headlined "Strong Stars" outlined how "Strong took a throw with his gloved hand on the initial sack and although the runner collided with him as he crossed the bag, it was the runner who got knocked down because Strong held the ball and kept his foot on the bag."[5]

The family was proud of the twenty-one-year-old, and he had only just scratched the surface in the American pastime. After the celebration and accolades subsided, it was back to work with his dad and the Indianapolis Athletics. Unfortunately, the team finished the first half of the season 9–18 and in second-to-last place in its division. What made matters worse, the team did not have a full season due to league financial problems. However, this did not stop Ted Jr. from enjoying one of the sports he loved. He took part in seven postseason games as a member of a combined team of the Chicago American Giants and Kansas City Monarchs of the newly formed Negro American League. This team played a team composed of the Homestead Grays and the Newark Eagles players from the Negro National League. From September 19–26, these two powerhouse squads played in various stadiums from Indianapolis and Pittsburgh to Philadelphia and Baltimore as the Homestead Grays and Newark Eagles combined team took six of the seven games.

Now that Ted Jr. was an adult, he could count on sports to make a decent living. With the 1937 baseball season over, he rejoined Abe Saperstein's Harlem Globetrotters and played guard on the heralded team. As a two-sport athlete, Ted Jr. realized that he could keep the monies flowing and see most of the country—a feat that most African Americans could only imagine.

In the meantime, his father kept busy in the sport he loved, too. Strong Sr. worked with the Indianapolis Athletics, later known as the ABCs, to keep the team afloat as a part of the Negro American League. At the annual spring meeting of the Negro American League owners and officials at the Appomattox Club in Chicago on February 19, 1938, Strong Sr. (identified as T. R. Strong, Indianapolis, in a *Chicago Defender* newspaper report) represented the Indianapolis ABCs in preparation for the 1938 season. The *Defender* story of the meeting reported that Strong Sr. was one of the managers present and introduced in the open meeting. The outcome of the meeting showed the leagues banding together to respect player agreements.

This show of solidarity was in direct response to Satchel Paige and other Negro Leagues players who accepted lucrative offers from owners of teams from other countries.[6]

4

THE SKY IS THE LIMIT

Ted Jr. ascended to heights that made him a recognized celebrity in the African American community. His outstanding play in the Negro Leagues prompted baseball fans to select him to play in the 1938 East-West All-Star Game at Comiskey Park in Chicago on August 21. He finished third in the balloting with 46,682 votes, behind Showboat Thomas with 59,938 and Jim West with 63,401. Ted Jr. remained among the cream of the crop in the African American sports world. He, like other African American athletes, was mentioned in conversations in barbershops and pool halls, but the big hoopla still held firm for Joe Louis, Satchel Paige, Henry Armstrong (who became the first professional boxer to hold three world titles at one time), and Jesse Owens (winner of four gold medals at the 1936 Olympics).

Nevertheless, Ted Jr. represented the Indianapolis ABCs at first base for the second consecutive year. More than thirty thousand fans were in the stands as the best of the best in the Negro Leagues were on the field. The lineup for both squads reflected the African American community's joy of baseball and knowledge of the players that hailed from the various cities in the United States:

East
Vic Harris (Homestead Grays), lf
Sammy T. Hughes (Baltimore Elite Giants), 2b
Willie Wells (Newark Eagles), ss
Buck Leonard (Homestead Grays), 1b
Rev Cannady (New York Black Yankees), 3b
Sam Bankhead (Pittsburgh Crawfords), cf
Bill Wright (Baltimore Elite Giants), rf
Biz Mackey (Baltimore Elite Giants), c

Edsall Walker (Homestead Grays), p
Barney Brown (New York Black Yankees), ph–p
Schoolboy Johnny Taylor (Pittsburgh Crawfords), p
Jake Dunn (Philadelphia Stars), ph

West
Henry Milton (Kansas City Monarchs), rf
Newt Allen (Kansas City Monarchs), 2b
Alec Radcliffe (Chicago American Giants), 3b
Ted Strong Jr. (Indianapolis ABCs), 1b
Quincy Trouppe (Indianapolis ABCs), lf
Neil Robinson (Memphis Red Sox), cf
Frank Duncan (Chicago American Giants), c
Parnell Woods (Birmingham Black Barons), ph
Larry Brown (Memphis Red Sox), c
Byron Johnson (Kansas City Monarchs), ss
Sug Cornelius (Chicago American Giants), p
Hilton Smith (Kansas City Monarchs), p
Ted Radcliffe (Memphis Red Sox), p

As with all of the East-West All-Star classics, the 1938 national show-case had all the trimmings. Chicago mayor Edward J. Kelly attended the game and threw out the ceremonial first pitch, albeit short of home plate as he claimed later that he "was a bit off form." The African American community dressed to impress, as was the nature of people during this time. A person had to dress "sharp" when appearing in public, and you could see some of the most stylish outfits of the day for both males and females at Comiskey Park that August afternoon.

This All-Star classic provided a number of thrills with *Chicago Defender* columnist and the first dean of African American baseball writers Frank A. "Fay" Young superbly capturing the most outstanding one:

> Thirty thousand fans, bordering on hysteria, all did a "Susie Q" Sunday afternoon at Comiskey Park in the home third of the sixth annual East versus West classic when Neil Robinson (Memphis Red Sox) slammed what should have been a single (or perhaps a double) to center field and Sam Bankhead (Pittsburgh Crawfords) let the ball go through him for a home run inside of the park—and away went the ball game.[1]

This time Ted Jr. and the West squad tasted their first All-Star victory, nip-ping the East 5–4. Ted Jr. scored a run and had one walk and three at bats with no hits. His fielding at first base bode well for a second-time all-star.

After the game, the African American press, which began in 1827 with *Freedom's Journal* published by John B. Russwurm and Samuel E. Cornish, argued the case "about the ability of the Negro players to make the big league grade."[2] Fay Young wrote in the September 24, 1938, national edition of the *Chicago Defender*,

> The consensus of opinion of the fans who watched the game [1938 East-West All-Star Game] is that there are several big league clubs who could use one or more of the sepia diamond performers . . . a combination of Negro Leagues players such as Buck Leonard, Homestead Grays, or Ted Strong, Indianapolis, at first; Willie Wells, Newark Eagles, manager, at short; Newt Allen, Kansas City Monarch captain, or Sammy Hughes, Baltimore, at second; Ray Dandridge, Newark or Walter Cannady, New York Black Yanks, at third; Josh Gibson, the Negro Babe Ruth who Waite Hoyt, former Yankee-Dodger hurler, says has the best throwing arm in anybody's league or Pepper Bassett of the Pittsburgh Crawfords behind the bat; Vic Harris, Homestead Grays, Bill Wright, Baltimore, and Robinson of the Memphis Red Sox in the outfield, would make it tough sledding for their big league opponents.

While the African American press lauded the ability of Negro Leagues players, the white press expressed doubts. An article titled, "How Good Is Negro Baseball?" by Lloyd Lewis in the *Chicago Daily News* on August 22, 1938, observed that "Negro professional baseball . . . is faster on the bases than the major league ball now being played in the American and National circuits; it is almost as swift and spectacular in the field; it lacks the batting form of the white man's big leagues." The reporter went on to criticize the play of Negro Leagues players during the East-West All-Star Game the day before, and he didn't miss a step in criticizing Ted Jr. for "showboating" with the glove:

> A trace of non-professionalism also cropped out here and there yesterday when fielders took throws on lines drives with one hand when two would have been safer. Strong, the tall, magnificently proportioned first baseman from the Indianapolis A.B.C.s insists upon "showboating" with his glove, a trick of vain glory, which he should forget even if one of his hands is as large as the average man's two. (He is a sensational basketball player in wintertime.)[3]

Ted Jr. wasn't a showboater. He knew he was good, and he displayed it every chance he got. With baseball season winding down, he plunged headlong into basketball. For more than ten years, the Globetrotters had barnstormed the country playing small-town all-star teams. It was now time to test the waters of professional basketball teams. In 1939, the first ever World Basketball Tournament was held at the Chicago Stadium, and the Harlem Globetrotters saw this as their opportunity to ascend to the big time. The lineup featured eight teams: Oshkosh All-Stars, Sheboygan Redskins, Original Celtics, New York Renaissance (also known as the Rens), Chicago Harmons, New York Yankees, House of David, and the Fort Wayne Harvesters.

Ted Jr. grew to six feet, four inches and weighed just over two hundred pounds. During this time in sports, he was considered a *big* man and Abe Saperstein moved him from guard to center. Ted Jr. led a team that included Bernie Price, forward; Harry Rusan, forward; Hillary Brown, forward; Babe Pressley, guard; Larry Bleach, guard; and Inman Jackson, guard. The team won its first game 41–33 over the Fort Wayne Harvesters and advanced to the second round on the evening of March 26, 1939. The Globetrotters reached the semifinal round by defeating the Chicago Harmons 31–25. Ted Jr. and his teammates were one win away from a World Basketball Championship. They were ready for the challenge even though most basketball pundits of the era didn't give them a chance against the favorites, the New York Renaissance, better known as the Rens. By 1939, New York City had become the mecca of professional basketball. The Rens defeated the top teams in the East. Their reputation had become well-known by people who paid attention to professional basketball.[4]

The National edition of the *Chicago Defender* covered the championship game:

> Both teams had advanced on Sunday afternoon and 10,000 were on hand to see the feature game. Even Bob Douglas, owner of the Rens, was here from New York.
>
> **Too Much Experience**
> It was simply a case of too much experience plus height and a stout defense. The Globe Trotters were no match for the Rens. Even the Globe Trotters' shots which rained off the glass backboard were erratic. Fats Jenkins, captain of the New York quintet was "in his sins." He rode little Captain Rusan until it was a joke. Rusan got one lone field goal.
>
> The star of the Globe Trotters was Larry Bleach, the Detroit policeman, who was captain of the Detroit university cage team. Bleach came through with three field goals. Strong was next with two. On the Rens, Smith connected for three baskets and dropped in two trys

from the free gift line. Tarzan Cooper and Jenkins got two field goals and two free tries.

The Rens were out in front at the half, 15 to 10, after leading the Globe Trotters 8 to 1, 9 to 2 and 11 to 2 in the early stages of the first half.

Trail by Two Points

Only once did it look like the Globe Trotters "might" become an inspired team and stop the campions [*sic*]. That was near the middle of the second half when baskets by Bleach, Pressley and Strong brought the Globe Trotters' total to 23 and they trailed the New Yorkers by two points.

The Rens got the ball and after some whirlwind passing, Cooper, loose under the basket, made the final shot of the night. At no time did the Globe Trotters get a chance to put on an exhibition of ball handling or passing. They were guarded so close that most of their shots were from a distance.[5]

The Rens defeated Ted Strong Jr. and the Globetrotters by the score of 27–23. In his first "World" Championship game, Ted Jr. scored three points, grabbed two rebounds, and missed two free throws. The Globetrotters knew they could have performed better, but they were up against an experienced opponent who showed them why they were the favorites going into the tournament. The defeat just made them hungrier for a rematch in 1940.

Ted Jr. and his teammates had the opportunity to hone their skills against opponents from small towns throughout the Midwest. They resumed the hectic playing schedule that allowed Ted Jr. to supplement his income and keep in shape for baseball season.

In February 1939, the Negro American League club owners held their spring meeting at the Appomattox Club in Chicago. Strong Sr. again represented the Indianapolis ABCs. At this meeting, the club owners approved team schedules and announced the playing of two East-West All-Star games. The first game was set for Chicago on August 8 with the second to be played in New York City at an undetermined date. Abe Saperstein, president of the Mid-West League, addressed the owners, the *Chicago Defender* reported. Saperstein and Strong Sr. may have exchanged pleasantries since Ted Jr. was the two-sports star whom many people praised.

Strong Sr. tried to keep tabs on his now-famous son. He knew the Globetrotters were becoming household names since losing gallantly to the New York Rens. As fame began to take Ted Jr. to heights unknown, his father worried that it was only a matter of time before the vices of life and sports would overtake his firstborn. "Ted was playing with the best of them," Strong Sr. said. "I tried hard to protect him as much as I could."[6]

By 1939, Strong Sr. and Vera had to manage a much larger Strong clan. According to Jasper Strong, who was born in 1934, there were eight mouths to feed. The 1940 Census documented only three children living at the Strong household at 4225 South Wabash Avenue. Ted Jr. was twenty-two years old and traveling the country with the Globetrotters and Negro Leagues baseball teams. Future Negro Baseball League star Othello Strong still resided with Mom and Dad.

Strong Sr. may have represented the Indianapolis ABCs at the winter Negro Leagues baseball meeting, but it is uncertain if he maintained a relationship with the team after the Mound City Blues, a team from southwestern Illinois, near St. Louis, became the representative organization for the team. The now Mound City Blues–Indianapolis ABCs didn't keep Ted Jr. and his good friend and teammate Quincy Trouppe for long. Trouppe, one of the Negro Baseball League's best catchers, joined a team in Monterrey, Mexico, and in April Ted Jr. was traded to the Kansas City Monarchs in exchange for Kansas City first baseman Eldridge Mayweather.[7]

Ted Jr. joined a Kansas City Monarchs team that was beginning to blossom as a standout team in the Negro Leagues. The Monarchs in the early 1930s were strictly a road club playing teams such as the House of David that brought in white players such as Grover Cleveland Alexander, Babe Didrikson, and Dizzy Dean's father as added attractions to get people to attend the games. In 1937, the team's management rejoined the newly created Negro American League.[8] For Ted Jr. it was probably a dream come true. Here he was a twenty-two-year-old joining the celebrated Monarchs, a team that "had the same meaning as the New York Yankees would have had for a boy forty years ago. Just to tell the fellas back home, very cool-like, mind you, 'Yeah, I'm going to be playing for the Kansas City Monarchs,' was quite a thrill. Quite a thrill. The Kansas City Monarchs."[9]

In 1938, the team finished second in the standings in the Negro American League. The prospects for 1939 were high when Ted Jr. took the reins at shortstop and worked to meld with the likes of right fielder Henry Milton, first baseman Buck O'Neil, and center fielder Turkey Stearnes. It is interesting how some of Ted Jr.'s teammates remember him. Buck O'Neil, who eventually became good friends with Ted Jr., fondly recalled:

> Ted Strong . . . was our shortstop, maybe the tallest shortstop ever to play the game. He was darn near seven feet tall, a switch-hitter with tremendous power—I saw him hit mammoth home runs from both

sides of the plate in one game. Ted was like Cal Ripken, only bigger. They put him at short because he had great hands and rifle arm. In fact, he was one of the first real tall guys who could do a lot of things. Now, of course, tall guys are all slick just like he was, but back then it was a shock.[10]

The 1939 season started out a little rocky for the Monarchs. On May 5, they lost a three-game series to the Homestead Grays, a team that featured home-run-hitting Josh Gibson and first baseman Buck Leonard. On May 19, they were defeated by the Memphis Red Sox 6–2 in a night game in Clarksdale, Mississippi, that was scheduled by Kansas City Monarchs owner J. L. Wilkinson. In this game Ted Jr. accounted for the Monarchs' only hit when he knocked "one over the right field fence and it was said that it was the longest drive ever witnessed in this park."[11]

The team continued to struggle when they faced the Chicago American Giants in Chicago. They lost three out of four games and barely won the finale 6–5 in extra innings on a chilly Monday afternoon, May 26.

In June, the Monarchs began to find their stride and the wins began to mount. On June 2 the team returned home to Ruppert Stadium and took a doubleheader from Ted Jr.'s former team, the Indianapolis ABCs, 3–0 and 9–4. Ted Jr. contributed with timely hits, a stolen base, and a base on balls. On June 9 the team grabbed a doubleheader from the St. Louis Stars, 4–2 and 4–3. In the first game, Ted Jr. tripled, driving in two runs. The Monarchs fought other contenders like the Chicago American Giants and the St. Louis Stars. On June 23 the team marched into Cleveland, Ohio, and split a doubleheader with the Cleveland Bears before a crowd of four thousand spectators who withstood chilly weather and drizzling rain. In the first game, the Monarchs shut out the Bears 11–0. Ted Jr. homered in the seventh inning with two on. In the second game, Cleveland prevailed and returned the favor with an 11–1 victory. In July the Monarchs returned home again to face the Chicago American Giants, who had given them trouble a month earlier. This time the confident Monarchs swept the Giants by scores of 9–4 and 6–3. The two teams squared off again for a double bill in early August, and the Monarchs handled the Giants 4–2 and 6–2. Ted Jr. and his teammates knew they had the Giants' number, and the *Chicago Defender* article expressed as much:

The Monarchs put as much into the third inning as is packed into any ordinary nine frames. Brown singled to center and went to second when Simms played with the ball. Strong hit to Bowe who got Brown at third on a nice throw to A. Radcliff. Strong stole second while Bowe was winding up. Strong then stole third, sliding under Radcliff who took Bowe's throw. Then came some baseball. Greene walked. Strong had home stolen when smart Newt Allen took a long chance, he bunted the third strike fair and was out Bowe to Gillard, but Strong got credit for the theft of home and Allen a sacrifice because his quick thinking put Greene on second.[12]

The Monarchs were rolling, and Ted Jr. had made his family proud. When the lineup for the August 6, 1939, seventh annual East-West All-Star Game was announced, Ted Jr. again was chosen. This time he led the all-star balloting as first baseman for the West squad with a total of 508,327 votes. (This vote total was the highest ever recorded for a player in the history of the East-West classic.) Ted Jr. was joined on the West squad by fellow Monarch players right fielder Henry Milton and pitcher Hilton Smith. Other stars included Alec Radcliffe of the Chicago American Giants and Ted "Double Duty" Radcliffe of the Memphis Red Sox.

Ted Jr. again tasted victory when the West defeated the East 4–2 before forty thousand fans at Comiskey Park. *Chicago Defender* sportswriter Fay Young did a marvelous job describing the game. His lead paragraph summarized the contest:

> In a game packed with thrills and before the most colorful and largest crowd ever to witness any athletic event of our group, the West won the 1939 East versus West annual baseball classic at Comiskey Park, Sunday, August 6.[13]

Ted Jr. probably had a bit of the jitters playing before forty thousand people. Heavyweight boxing champion Joe Louis attended the game with his wife, his co-manager, and a bodyguard. The champion, dressed in a white gabardine suit and looking well-groomed and tanned after playing eighteen holes of golf, pitched the first ball and received a tremendous ovation. The weather was ideal at the start of the 3:00 p.m. game, and Ted Jr. knew his family was in the crowd cheering him on. He had two at bats, no hits, and one error, which was described by Fay Young: "Then Strong took Buck Leonard's grounder and played with it like a kitten with a rubber ball and the great Homestead Gray's first sacker reached first safely."[14]

One saving grace involved the play of Ted Jr.'s teammate Hilton Smith. In relief, Smith pitched the fourth, fifth, and sixth innings and didn't allow a hit. Another saving grace was that Ted Jr. was selected to the second All-Star Game that the Negro Leagues established to allow more fans to enjoy the classic in the eastern United States. In this game, played in Yankee Stadium on Sunday, August 27, Ted Jr. joined fellow Monarch right fielder Turkey Stearnes and pitcher Hilton Smith in doing battle against an East squad that contained home-run-hitting Homestead Grays catcher Josh Gibson. This time Ted Jr. and the West fell to the East 10–2. Gibson blasted a triple with the bases loaded and hit a four-hundred-foot sacrifice fly that "was just short of being a homer to score the first East run in the opening frame."[15] Ted Jr. had four at bats with one hit. Attendance for the game was twenty thousand, although several African American sportswriters disputed the number of people in attendance and blamed the lack of publicity by the Negro Leagues owners as one of the reasons for the low turnout.

The Monarchs sprinted to the championship of the Negro American League in September and won three out of five games against the St. Louis Stars. Ted Jr. played on his first baseball championship team. He had ascended to heights that many young African American men his age could only dream of. He was tall, well-built, fun-loving, and well-known throughout the African American communities in Kansas City, Missouri, and Chicago. The opposite sex couldn't help but notice such an outstanding athlete, and he eventually met a young woman who caught his eye. Her name was Ruth H. Jackson, and she came from the Kansas City, Missouri, area.

While in Kansas City with the Monarchs, Ted Jr. accomplished another landmark in his life. On September 2, 1939, he obtained marriage license number A76094 from the Recorder of Deeds of Jackson County, Missouri, and he married Ruth. The marriage application indicated that Ted Jr. was twenty-five and Ms. Jackson was twenty-eight. There appeared to be a bit of a mix-up—at that time, Ted Jr. would have been twenty-two years old. Whether it was intentional or not, Strong Sr. always said, "Ted was big for his age."

The Monarchs closed the season at Ward Field in Kansas City, Kansas, with a twin victory against the Satchel Paige All-Stars. Ted Jr. continued to shine as "brilliant defense by Strong at shortstop on two chances held the runner at third and the side was retired on an easy out to the pitcher."[16]

Ted Jr. returned to Chicago to visit with family and friends with a Negro Leagues Championship under his belt and a new bride. "We would have a good time when Ted and Othello would come to the house," Jasper Strong reminisced. "All of our family members would come by and we all would enjoy my mother's cooking. They would play cards and talk way into the wee hours."[17] Jasper Strong was just four years old during this time in 1939. He doesn't remember his brother's first wife.

As the year 1939 moved to a close, Ted Jr.'s athletic stock continued on an upward trajectory. Earlier that year his Harlem Globetrotters finished third in the World Basketball Championships. He was selected to his third-straight All-Star Game, and he played on the Negro American League Kansas City Monarchs championship baseball team. One can only speculate that his financial situation was better than the average African American during this time. And he was about to turn twenty-three years old in January 1940.

5

PRIME TIME ABOUNDS WITH HICCUPS

Ted Jr.'s visit with friends and family, and any honeymoon with his new bride, were cut short by the rigors of the Harlem Globetrotters' schedule. The Globetrotters of the late 1920s through the early 1940s were professional basketball players striving to prove that they were one of the world's best professional teams. In essence, teams like the Globetrotters, the Rens, and others were the forerunners of the National Basketball Association (NBA). The Globetrotters played to win games, but they also knew that to keep the interest of the fans, since they were defeating local teams with ease, they had to "entertain" the fans. That's when "shadow-ball" came into existence. According to Strong Sr., shadow-ball was a way to show off basketball skills. It was a spin-off from what was done in the Negro Baseball Leagues.

"We would go through different mimics and sleight of hand [with the baseball] and this was very acceptable. This we did in road trips with baseball. . . . We set up and made it plausible for people to come out. . . . Most came out to see us perform than to see us to play ball because we put on a show," Strong Sr. commented.[1]

Ted Jr. and his teammates, along with Saperstein, figured that demonstrating what they could do with a basketball while defeating their local community opponents handily would be a successful ploy to keep people coming to the games. When the Globetrotters played in Ogden, Utah, on Christmas night 1939, the *Ogden Standard-Examiner* wrote:

Harlemites To Play Double Header Thursday
New Yorkers Show Marvelous Ability Against All-Stars
Colored Wizards Pronounced Greatest Team Ever
To Show In Ogden; Open Date Makes It Possible
to Reschedule Famous Team

Abe Saperstein's Harlemites, acclaimed champions of the basketball world, are still champions. The large crowd which saw the invaders remove all doubt from the Ogden All-Stars' minds at the Weber gym Christmas night clamored for more, so they'll be brought back Thursday evening.

Popular demand will bring the Globetrotters back, back to attempt the iron man stunt of beating two teams in one evening.

The New Yorkers had everything Christmas night, winning as they pleased over the All-Stars, 54 to 45. The score could have been doubled, tripled or more had the world titleholders chosen to "lay it on." Saperstein's team sent the fans and All-Stars out the Weber gym Christmas night literally talking to themselves. All agreed that this team was the best that ever invaded Ogden.

That's not pulling a punch.

A great star in every position, two of the Trotters were of the sensational variety: Ted Strong and Inman Jackson.

Two Stars

Jackson gave the fans a marvelous performance of ball handling. The All-Stars swarmed over him in twos and threes, but failed to pry the ball loose.

This chap Ted Strong has the largest hands in the game. He is the only man who can reach and snatch the ball in mid-air with the fingers of one hand. It's one of the miracles of the sport to see Strong catch a pass or stop a dribble in this manner.[2]

The wins continued to mount as the Globetrotters toured the country preparing themselves for the World Basketball Championships in March 1940. In Helena, Montana, the *Helena Daily Independent* on February 28 reported:

A large crowd of Helena basketball fans saw one of the greatest exhibitions of basketball finesse ever presented in the west when the Harlem Globetrotters delighted them with a wonderful show that included a 59-27 victory over the Y.M.C.A. All Stars. . . .

This is one of the most competent teams A. M. Saperstein has sent on the road. Headed by the brilliant Ted Strong, the negro basketeers lived up to every advance notice when they took time out from serious basketball, which was over half of the time, and decided to play a few tricks, they had the crowd in an uproar. As ball handlers they have no peer and the crowd really saw some brilliant basket throwing as well as the comedy.[3]

As the team headed into March, they were ready for the challenge of winning what had eluded them a year before: the World's Basketball Championship. For Ted Jr. the world championship was similar to playing a home game since the tournament would be held in Chicago this time. The *Chicago Herald-American* newspaper sponsored the tournament slated to begin March 17. Fourteen teams were invited from around the country. Among the teams vying for the title was the reigning champion New York Renaissance. The 1940 Globetrotters entered the tournament as an independent and the featured "traveling team" since they had "played the best teams in the country and defeated them regularly."[4]

In an article in the national edition of the *Chicago Defender* on March 9, 1940, Ted Jr. is prominently mentioned in an obvious news release from the Globetrotters:

> One of the featured performers is Ted Strong, captain and center of the team, who is well known as a baseball performer. Strong played first base for the Kansas City Monarchs last year and led the American league in hitting with an average of .403.[5]

Ted Jr. and teammates opened the tournament against the Kenosha Royals on Sunday, March 17, at the 132nd Regiment Armory at Madison and Rockwell streets and won handily 50–26. The next day the Globetrotters met the team that denied them the championship the previous year, the New York Renaissance, or Rens. The Rens had remained a powerhouse squad, and this game became one of the hottest ticket events of the year. More than nine thousand people jammed into the Armory for the quarterfinal game, which had been scheduled to tip off at 10:30 p.m. When the earlier game went into overtime, Ted Jr. and teammates didn't take the floor until after 11:00 p.m.

It has been written that the flashy and confident world champion Rens intimidated the Globetrotters during the team warm-ups. Confidence the Globetrotters didn't lack. Anticipation made them nervous, and only a slap in the face would bring them back to reality that they were the sole team capable of defeating the Rens. The slap back to reality came from one of the original members of the team, Inman Jackson. He knew the glitter and gold the Rens were flashing could mesmerize the best athletes on any given night. He gave a pep talk shaking his teammates from their momentary stage fright.[6] Maybe the nine thousand spectators gave the team the jitters, but Ted Jr. and teammates were veterans, having been with the Globetrotters since the early 1930s. Despite the late hour start and the early jitters, the Globetrotters defeated the Rens 37–36 when Sonny Boswell sank two free throws with forty seconds left.

On the afternoon of Tuesday, March 19, the Globetrotters defeated the Syracuse Reds 34–24 in the semifinals while George Halas's Chicago Bruins defeated the Heurich Beers of Washington, D.C., in the other semifinal contest. The Globetrotters were at the threshold of their first world championship. Although the Globetrotters were based in Chicago, they played the majority of their games on the road. One local newspaper called the Globetrotters "that phenomenal sepia quintet from Seattle, Washington."[7] The Chicago Bruins were considered the hometown favorites. The Globetrotters were also considered the underdogs to the Bruins, who defeated other teams with ease.

The championship game between the Globetrotters and the Bruins seesawed with six lead changes and three tied scores. The Globetrotters' strong defense bottled up the Bruins until the middle of the third quarter when Ted Jr. fouled out of the game. Inman Jackson replaced him at center. Opinions flourished regarding Ted Jr.'s exit from the game. Many felt that insignificant fouls were called on Ted Jr. Up until he exited, the team had excellent rhythm and flow.[8] Ted Jr.'s teammates pulled together, as they had done all season, and fought to tie the game at 29. Ted Jr.'s good friend and childhood buddy, Bernie Price, scored the winning basket when he let loose a shot from the center of the court.[9] The Globetrotters did it. They were the World Professional Basketball Champions.

In addition to earning the title "World's Champions," the Globetrotters team received $1,000 prize money and a $1,000 contract to play a team of college all-stars at the Chicago Stadium in November 1940, and each team member received a $100 bonus check from Saperstein in addition to their regular paycheck.

"I was right there at Chicago Stadium," said ninety-four-year-old Timuel D. Black Jr., a prominent Chicago civil rights activist and noted historian. "The fact that they were going to be playing for the championship was momentous to the South Side, not just young people but for older people, too."[10]

But Mr. Black had his own reasons for being proud of Ted Jr. He remembered Ted Jr. from the Wendell Phillips High School days:

I remember Ted Strong when he performed in Captain Walter Henri Dyett's "High Jinx" variety show.[11] He sang the song "Shoe Shine Boy." Ted had a marvelous voice. He sung the song in the same spirit and elegance with his own voice as a Louis Armstrong singing that song. We were fascinated by this guy who was such a good athlete also being able to sing and perform. As he sang he was performing like a shoeshine boy. As he was singing he was strokin' a shoe.

Those of my generation cherish and remember Ted and his contemporaries of that period. They were not that much older but they were like big brothers. And Ted playing baseball . . . he could hit a ball . . . oh, man. If we were playing in Phillips play yard, he could hit the ball and break someone's window a block away . . . and he did! So those memories or experiences were inspirational to those of us who were less talented and somewhat younger. He was a hero to those of us who remember Ted Strong.[12]

A feeling of jubilation was realized by Ted Jr.'s family and friends. The Reverend Morris Gordon, a childhood friend of Othello who idolized Ted Jr. and his Globetrotter teammates, reminisced:

We were so proud of them. We used to sneak up to Ted's room and get his Globetrotter jacket and wear it around the neighborhood. Bernie Price was the nicest guy you would ever meet. I remember when he came out to the vacant lot where we were playing basketball and played with us in his street clothes. Man, did we get a kick out of that. Here he is a professional athlete coming out in his street clothes to play with us and show us some moves.[13]

The Strong family probably celebrated with family and friends at Strong Sr.'s house at 4819 Langley Avenue, a complex consisting of a six-flat building housing a number of African American families, including Rev. Gordon, who lived next to the Strongs. The celebration went long into the night after the Globetrotters won the championship. Typically, in a six-flat building, families would open the doors of their apartments and friends and families walked the halls sampling food from each apartment since the mothers probably prepared a nice spread for all to enjoy. Apartment residents played music and people danced, sang, and had a great time. People in the neighborhood stopped by the complex to join in the celebration and congratulate Ted Jr. and other members of the Globetrotters who stopped by after being encouraged to do so by Strong Sr. and other friends and associates.

After several days of relaxing and letting the victory soak in, Ted Jr. needed to get back to work. Now that the Globetrotters were World

Champions, other teams around the country wanted their shot to defeat the champions. Moreover, Ted Jr. had to get ready for baseball season with the Negro American League Champion Kansas City Monarchs, who were looking forward to defending their championship.

From March 30 to April 5, 1940, the Globetrotters were in Bismarck, North Dakota, and surrounding areas to face the semiprofessional Bismarck Phantoms in a three-game series, which the champs won easily. However, contrary to published reports, Ted Jr. and Sonny Boswell did not join the team.

Apparently after the celebration subsided, the issue of money surfaced. Ted Jr. was to report to Marshall, Texas, to join his Monarch teammates in preparing for the upcoming baseball season. It was reported that Ted Jr. and other players had jumped their contracts with the Kansas City Monarchs and gone to Mexico to play.

To the person on the street, Ted Jr. and other Negro Leagues players lived a good life. People in the know knew otherwise. On many occasions, players would provide their baseball services on the field and after their job was done, pay for services rendered was not delivered. When opportunities for a paycheck materialized, like anyone, Ted Jr. followed the money in order to make a living.[14]

Ted Jr. was one of those players quietly complaining about pay conditions even though he had the Globetrotters income to supplement the baseball money shortage. But Ted Jr. and the other Globetrotters and baseball players knew that Negro Leagues baseball owners used their financial resources to pay someone like Abe Saperstein to handle publicity in the daily papers. It was reported that Saperstein received five percent of the receipts of a game where thirty-three thousand people paid. The players and outspoken Newark Eagles co-owner Mrs. Abe Manley couldn't understand why the majority of the owners wouldn't take care of the players first and handle matters like publicity in-house.

Being a star of the league, Ted Jr. didn't escape the pen of sports columnist Fay Young. An event happened where Ted Jr. received money from the owner of the Monarchs to travel to join the team in New Orleans. Due to a family illness, Ted Jr. reported late for a game in New Orleans, and he was taken to Mobile where he played in one game. Supposedly, a Monarch teammate persuaded Ted Jr. to go to Mexico for a greater payday. Apparently, the columnist wanted to show that not receiving pay for services rendered cut both ways. When Ted Jr. left the Monarchs, he played baseball as a member of the Nueva La Junta team in Monterrey, Mexico.

He led the Mexican League with twenty-two home runs and seventeen triples and "proved to be the best third baseman in the circuit."[15]

After completing the baseball season in Mexico and receiving compensation for his efforts, Ted Jr. journeyed back to the States to join his Globetrotter teammates on November 22 in Sheboygan, Wisconsin, and train with the Sheboygan Redskins of the National Pro League for the scheduled big game with the College All-Stars on November 29, 1940. Ted Jr.'s athletic physique impressed the sports reporter of the local newspaper:

> The 23-year-old husky, who formerly played with the Chicago American Giants and Kansas City Monarchs, appearing in several of the East-West baseball classics stands 6 feet, 3½ inches and has tremendous hands.[16]

Following the scrimmage with the Sheboygan Redskins, the Globetrotters traveled to Chicago to meet the College All-Stars on Friday, November 29. Why was a game between the Globetrotters and the College All-Stars so important? In those days professional sports were not on the pedestal that they are today. College sports held center court, and many of the college teams starred outstanding athletes with professional-level skills. In order to retain badly needed scholarships, athletes remained in college and maintained their amateur status.

Some sports historians maintain that Saperstein arranged the game with the College All-Stars to increase the Globetrotters' fan appeal. The evening of Friday, November 29, 1940, did bring more notoriety to Ted Jr. and his teammates.

The media reports depicted a game so exciting that readers must have wished they'd had tickets:

> Wow! What a game and what a finish was the history making basketball game between the World's Professional Champions Harlem Globe Trotters and College All Stars at the Chicago stadium, Friday night, November 29, before a hysterical crowd of 22,000 wild-eyed cheering cage fans. The Chicago Herald-American sponsored the game.
>
> With two minutes left to play, the Globe Trotters were leading 37 to 35 and "putting on the show" to kill time. The All Stars intercepted the ball and worked it down the floor like lightning with Carpenter of East Texas Teachers finally sinking the tying basket. This was the seventh time the score had been tied and before the end of the game it was tied twice more.

Following Carpenter's basket, Ralph Vaughn of U.S.C. put the All Stars in the lead, 39 to 37, with three seconds to play seeming to give his team the victory.

Passing the ball in from out of bounds following the basket, the Globe Trotters had but one thing to do, shoot and tie the score. And that is just what they did.

The ball went to Sonny Boswell who had 13 points to his credit already who let go and all the ball touched was the bottom of the basket, sending the game into overtime and the crowd wild.

The five minutes which were to be played in the overtime were filled with action. Boswell was fouled, sinking the free throw to put the Globe Trotters ahead 40 to 39. Vaughn again came through for the All Stars sinking a short shot to take the lead, 41 to 40; Erwin Prasse of Iowa was fouled and sank the free throw to increase the All Stars lead to 42 to 40. At this point it looked very bad for the Trotters but Louis Pressley came through, just as he had on four earlier occasions, to tie the score, 42 to 42, with less than a minute to play.

Then with all 22,000 fans on their feet cheering themselves hoarse, Stan Szukala of DePaul and co-captain of the team, crowned himself with glory when he cut sharply toward the basket from the right side and sank the game winning basket.

Thus did the great Globe Trotters go down, 44 to 42, and even in defeat they lost not one bit of their reputation, putting on displays of passing and ball handling that were uncanny and presenting one of the game's greatest shots in Sonny Boswell. If anything they should draw more this year than ever before.[17]

Playing the center position for the Globetrotters in the 1940s wasn't the glamour job that it came to be decades later. Ted Jr. grabbed rebounds, blocked shots, and anchored the defense. He didn't score in the game, but he contributed to the professionals' ability to keep the game close throughout the contest.

Saperstein's strategy of challenging the College All-Stars worked. Not only did the "loss" to the College All-Stars make the Globetrotters a must-see performance, it made Ted Jr. and teammates drawing cards in the Saperstein publicity and marketing machine. A short time after the College All-Star Game, the Saperstein marketing machine fed press releases about upcoming games to local newspaper outlets where the Globetrotters were scheduled to appear. One example was the *Ogden Standard-Examiner*, where on Sunday, January 26, 1941, the newspaper's staff writer used biographical sketches from a Harlem Globetrotter news release to announce an upcoming appearance by the team:

No basketball team in history can match the wonder record of the Harlem Globetrotters, world's champions, who meet the Ogden Pioneers, crack independent team, at the Ogden high school gymnasium the night of February 5.[18]

The news release described Ted Jr.:

TED STRONG . . . Center. Strong, playing his fifth season with the "Trotters" has improved faster than any man in the county at his position. A former star with Morgan College in Baltimore, he plays both basketball and baseball. He broke into negro professional baseball with the Chicago American Giants five seasons ago, and has since played with the Indianapolis A's and the Kansas City Monarchs. Considered the best young first baseman in the Negro American league, he led the circuit hitting last year with a mark of .403. He has been selected on the circuit's last three all-star teams. He is reputed to have the largest hands in basketball. He stands 6 feet, 3½ inches and weighs 210. Home city, South Bend, Ind.[19]

Ted Jr. consistently appeared in newspaper articles around the country as one of the selling attractions for the Harlem Globetrotters. Publicity photographs showed Ted Jr. and fellow Globetrotters under headlines crafted to entice readers:

Sell-Out Crowd To See Famed Globe Trotters
Colored Stars Move in
From Cincinnati Game;
Inman Jackson Top Man

The hectic schedule by the now "famed" Harlem Globetrotters kept Ted Jr. away from home quite often.

"They were always gone," said Rev. Gordon. "But we were extremely happy to see them when they came home. They were our heroes."[20]

Throughout 1941 the war in Europe and the spread of Nazi Germany consumed the attention of the American public. Ted Jr. and his teammates were hawked to many municipalities that wanted to take a shot at playing the world champions. His reputation was at an all-time high, and the Globetrotters publicity barrage pumped local newspapers with tidbits about the "Globetrotter Ace."

The *Cumberland Evening Times* of Cumberland, Maryland, on February 26, 1941, featured the following:

Globetrotters' Strong
Mixture of Great Stars

Six-Three 210-Pound Giant has developed into outstanding performer Big Ted Strong, a "hefty combination of 'Pepper' Martin and Jimmy Foxx, with maybe a little of Joe Louis thrown in," as one sports writer characterized him, will be manning one of the posts when the Harlem Globetrotters, world's champion basketball team opposes the North End Social and Athletic Club cagers on the SS. Peter & Paul school court next Sunday night at 9:30.

"Strong is vigorous and headlong like Martin, rugged like Foxx and overwhelming like Louis," explained the news-hawk in his analysis of the great athlete.

The six-foot-three-inch giant has led the famous Trotters to top renown, yet up to four years ago he never had a basketball in his hands. He came into the game through his baseball heroics, and by accident, at that.

Strong was playing baseball a few years back for the Chicago American Giants, and sports pages knew him as a terror. Vicious, at times almost foolhardy, he bowled 'em over the bases and knocked out home runs in an awkward but effective style. He also scooped up wicked grounders at third base with his bare hands.

The manager of the Globetrotters, A. M. Saperstein, noted Strong's enormous hands and give him a tryout that winter.

So rapidly has Ted mastered the sport, many now rate him as the greatest player in the game today. Last March, in the final game of the world's tournament in Chicago wherein the Globetrotters won their title, the South Bend, Ind., husky stopped big Mike Nuvak, of the Chicago Bruins, cold. Lee Edwards of Oshkosh, who led the American Pro League in scoring three straight years, left a game weeping because he looked like an amateur along-side Strong, who held him to two points.

Last summer Ted played baseball in Mexico as a member of the LaJunta team at Monterrey. All he did was lead the league in home runs, triples and just about everything else.

This is Strong's fifth season and the 210-pound giant is rapidly developing into one of the best ball handlers in the game. He has also played baseball with the Indianapolis A. B. C.'s and the Kansas City Monarchs in the Negro American League. In his first five seasons of negro professional baseball he was selected on three all-star teams. Playing with the Monarchs, Strong topped the league in hitting in 1938 with .403.[21]

The public relations arm of Saperstein's Globetrotter enterprise released these "tidbits" of information to build the hype that brought patrons to the basketball games. At times the PR writers took liberties with the truth. In the above story, Ted Jr. had played basketball at Wendell Phillips High School and quietly with Saperstein's pre-Harlem Globetrotters team. Actually, Ted Jr. learned the games of baseball and basketball from his father and guys in his neighborhood.

The fact that Ted Jr. could "control the paint" and shut down many "big" men of his era was nothing but the truth. It would be only a matter of time before Ted Jr. would demonstrate again that he was a force to be reckoned with in professional basketball.

The Globetrotters continued their tremendous play around the country. They were so popular that Saperstein created Western and Eastern "units" or teams to cover the requests to see the world champions from cities across the country.

Ted Jr. made the circuit with the Globetrotters to generate income and for the love of the game. As world champions, the Globetrotters had a big target on their backs. They were playing teams that included eminent college athletes, and the local press wrote glowing reports about what fans could expect when the Globetrotters came to town. These games helped the team prepare to defend their title in the 1941 World Professional Basketball Tournament slated for March 15–19 at the nine-thousand-seat Chicago International Amphitheatre, 42nd and Halsted Street in Chicago. The Globetrotters seldom had days off. Saperstein consistently had one of the units playing somewhere in the country. In his "I Cover The Eastern Front," *Chicago Defender* columnist Eddie Gant noted that the Globetrotters were scheduled to tour the East Coast, appearing in Washington, D.C., on March 4 and Baltimore on March 5, and that the team was "awaited along the eastern seaboard with high anxiety by basketball followers" since the Globetrotters had defeated the "world famous Renaissance last year for the world championship."[22]

The basketball followers would have to wait. Saperstein and the Globetrotters knew a bigger chance at stardom awaited them later in the year as the teams were among the sixteen squads, representing a cross-section of the United States, lining up to do battle for the championship.

The stage was set, and the twenty-four-year-old Ted Jr. and his teammates were ready to face the supreme test. For the second year in a row, the Globetrotters opened the tournament with the press hyping the fact that they would be facing a formidable opponent. Again, the Rens were touted as a superior team with stars such as former Long Island University standout William "Dolly" King, who was "rated as one of the three greatest Negro athletes in the world."[23]

The Globetrotters defeated their first-round opponent 38–29. In this game, Ted Jr. played forward while his good friend Bernie Price played center. Ted Jr. scored two points in the winning effort.

Ted Jr.'s neighborhood was again buzzing with the anticipation of another championship. Residents young and old in the South Side neighborhood never tired of hearing of the exploits of their champions. In between games, Ted Jr. often found time to visit and talk with neighborhood friends.

"They were glad to talk to people they knew," said Chicago childhood neighbor Tim Black. "They showed us that it was possible to overcome the impossible . . . racial barriers. I had fond memories of Ted Strong as a gentleman in terms of his social style. To us he was great because he was an example of what could be accomplished," Black added.[24]

In the quarterfinal round against the Detroit Eagles, Ted Jr. played forward with Sonny Boswell, Bernie Price at center, and Louis "Babe" Pressley and Duke Cumberland at guard. The game started with the champions leading for three-quarters of the game. The strain of a long, hard season began to take its toll. In the fourth quarter, the Eagles came from behind and nipped the Globetrotters 37–36. Ted Jr. and his teammates may have succumbed to the grueling season they experienced; however, to generate sufficient revenue, Saperstein booked games, and time off before the big tournament was out of the question. Shortly after the Globetrotters lost, the press reported the following:

Globe Trotters Visit Night Spots—And Lose

The Harlem Globe Trotters disappointed many of their followers by their poor performance in the world pro cage championship tourney. Although this aggregation, which was defending its title, won from the Newark, N. Y. (not New Jersey) Elks team, the game was considered sloppy by close followers of the sport.

The Globe Trotters dropped a 37 to 36 game to the Detroit Eagles on Sunday night. It was in the last few minutes of this game that the Globe Trotters looked anything like the world championship team of 1940.

There was a reason. The public ought to know so here it is: (1) Some of the Globe Trotters were at Dave's café, a popular night spot, enjoying themselves at the Gay Octette's cabaret party of Friday night and were seen there until the rays of the morning sun were breaking over Lake Michigan. Their opponents were asleep in bed. (2) Some of the Globe Trotters were seen past the hour of midnight Saturday at the Brass Rail. Their opponents were asleep in bed. [25]

The article/editorial continued with criticism of the Globetrotters' style of play during a recent tour of the East Coast where they lost to the New York Rens and attributed their defeat to the fact that "the westerners were forced to play eastern rules." Whether or not the Globetrotters actually partied the night away on Friday night, they played two games on Monday, March 17, not Sunday, March 16. The first game was played in the afternoon against the Newark Elks and the second against the Detroit Stars in the evening, where they lost by one point.

A combination of factors contributed to the Globetrotters' loss of the world champion title. First, a punishing traveling basketball schedule intended to generate revenue for owner Saperstein undoubtedly took a toll on the players. Second, the Globetrotters may have been overconfident; they were racking up wins against some of the nation's best professional and semiprofessional basketball teams. Why not relax and enjoy yourself a couple of days before you begin tournament play? You are at home, not on the road, and you will have a day or so to recover in order to compete. And maybe the Detroit Eagles were just a great basketball team in 1941. They defeated the 1939 world champion New York Rens in the semifinal round and then became the 1941 world champions by trouncing the Oshkosh All-Stars in the finals.

Regardless, it is understandable that many Chicagoans, especially in the Black Belt, were disappointed. The Globetrotters were a huge source of pride in the Black Belt, especially when sources of inspiration were not all that common. Even though Ted Jr. and teammates didn't finish in the top three, professional basketball was, after all, a business for Saperstein, and the team just brushed off the defeat, licked its wounds, and resumed its ambitious touring schedule.

While Ted Jr. and teammates were battling for the world championship, Negro Leagues baseball owners met to lay the groundwork for the 1941 season. This meeting would be of great interest to Ted Jr. and other players who had jumped their contracts to play in Mexico or Venezuela. A joint meeting of the Negro National and American League owners at the Hotel Grand in Chicago on Sunday, February 23, decided the fate of Ted Jr. and the other players. This decision was not an easy one. Some of the owners were upset that some players who jumped their contracts were being allowed back in the league. The meeting appeared to be heading for disaster until one of the owners motioned to amend the league's three-year ban on jumping players. A grace period was enacted allowing players to return to their respective teams. The motion passed easily.[26]

For Ted Jr., the decision to rejoin the Kansas City Monarchs by mid-April was not difficult. He loved baseball and rejoining the 1940 reigning champions with distinguished ballplayers such as Buck O'Neil, Newt Allen, Satchel Paige, and Hilton Smith made sense. Moreover, there was another way of looking at the "jumping" of contracts. How could you pass up the opportunity to make double or triple what you were paid in the Negro Leagues? And, when you couple this with the freedom from Jim Crow laws and living life and being treated as human beings, Latin American countries were the paradise that most African Americans in the 1930s and 1940s could only imagine:

> Despite the cultural differences, life in the Latin American countries was more "Norman." Black ballplayers did not have to play three games a day; they did not have to sleep in busses as they jounced to another town. On the ball field they played against and with white major leaguers such as Early Wynn, Mickey Owen, Sal Maglie, Max Lanier, Whitey Ford, and Tommy Lasorda. And they competed as equals. Away from the ball field they were also treated as equals—eating in the same restaurants, staying at the same fine hotels, and basking in the same hero's glory.[27]

Overall, Ted Jr. had that competitive spirit he inherited from his father. He wanted to win, and he knew that some of his Monarch teammates would understand that a man had to do what a man had to do to survive.

Ted Jr. and his Monarch teammates got off to a marvelous start by taking two games from the Birmingham Black Barons in Birmingham, Alabama, in early May. The team went into its home opener on May 25 at Ruppert Stadium before a crowd of fourteen thousand and defeated the Memphis Red Sox 7–6. Ted Jr. just picked up where he left off in Mexico. In the sixth inning, he cracked a home run that sailed "over the fence in right field 375 feet from home plate to score Greene ahead of him."[28]

As the season progressed, Ted Jr. continued his spectacular play. He started the season playing third base for the Monarchs but was switched to right field. The fans noted Ted Jr.'s success and immediately voted him to the 1941 East-West All-Star contest. Ted Jr. and his family and friends were proud to see him recognized in the June 28 edition of the *Chicago Defender* sports section.

Ted Jr. and the Monarchs continued their march to defend their 1940 crown the following day, June 29, by taking a twin bill, 3–1 and 10–2, from the New York Black Yanks at Ruppert Stadium. Ted Jr. showed the fans why he was worthy of their All-Star ballot as he hit, ran, and scored runs that helped to bring victories for the Monarchs.

Ted Jr. had every right to revel in the notoriety and prestige he received as a standout in the Negro Leagues and as a professional basketball player with the Globetrotters. Each industry was ascending to great heights in the African American community, albeit baseball faster than basketball. Author Larry Lester, in his book about the Negro Leagues, named the East-West All-Star Game "the biggest sporting event in black America,"[29] barring a Joe Louis fight.

The African American community across the country struggled to recover from the ravages of the Great Depression. Because of Jim Crow and racism, African Americans had to turn to each other to survive. They strived to develop businesses and institutions to serve an underserved population. While it has been written and said that Negro Leagues baseball was a "rag-time" operated entity, many in the African American community knew otherwise. Mrs. Effa Manley, joint owner of the Newark Eagles, provided an overview of the then two Negro Baseball Leagues, the Negro American League operating in the West and the Negro National League operating in the East. In the July 19, 1941, national edition of the *Chicago Defender*, she described the baseball operations' process and explained that operating a Negro Leagues baseball venture cost approximately $480,000 annually, demonstrating that Negro business entities, despite the negative economic position they worked in, could excel. Mrs. Manley wrote:

> The season is short, running only from May to September, over this period each club spends about $40,000 operating. This large amount of money is spent for salaries, park rents, government taxes, equipment, transportation, balls, bats, etc. Multiply this by 12 and add some of the exhibition promotions, the baseball club spends a half million dollars a year, and it is just starting to grow. It will not only supply many jobs, but is something my race can feel proud of.
>
> The interest in Negro baseball is growing very definitely. There is of course room for improvement, but it is true of many things. Negroes as athletes are definitely tops. I honestly feel if our Negro ball players could get the care and attention ball players should have, if their lives could be made as easy and luxurious as the white ball players, you would see balls hit further, men run faster, and in general, see baseball that has never been played.[30]

The popularity of Negro Leagues baseball and Ted Jr.'s notoriety made the Strong family home a wonderful gathering place between games and seasons. Strong Sr. moved the family to 4819 Langley in the Black Belt, and a number of his children were reaching their teenage years. The U.S. Census of 1940 indicated that Nathaniel, Olivia, and Othello were eighteen, fifteen, and fourteen years old, respectively. This census, however, was not accurate. The Strong family also included Charlotte, twelve; Gwen, twelve; Dorothy, ten; Jasper, six; and Tyrone, four.

Jasper Strong recalled, "Oh, I probably met so many people as a youngster. My brother [Ted Jr.] would always stop by when he was in town. My dad would take us all to the games, especially the All-Star games," he recalled.[31]

With the 1941 All-Star Game on the horizon, everyone looked forward to the event. Ted Jr. and the Monarchs kept mowing down Negro Leagues opponents. On July 25 the Monarchs, with Satchel Paige on the mound, defeated the Cuban Stars at Yankee Stadium in front of 27,500 baseball fans, with Ted Jr. carving out two singles and scoring twice in the victory.

Ted Jr. and the Monarchs cruised into the 1941 East-West All-Star Game, and he joined fellow Monarch players shortstop Newt Allen, pitcher Hilton Smith, and pitcher Satchel Paige as members of the West squad. The Strong family was undoubtedly among the fifty thousand in attendance on the extremely hot and muggy Sunday afternoon on July 27 at Comiskey Park in Chicago. Ted Jr. garnered 176,806 votes and placed fifth behind the top vote getter for outfielders, Dan Wilson of the St. Louis Stars with 197,503.

This game drew the largest crowd ever to witness the All-Star classic, and the excitement in the air was electric. The East squad jumped to the lead on Ted Jr. and his West teammates in the first inning. Batting left-handed in the West's half of the first inning, Ted Jr. didn't waste time responding as he smashed a double to left field scoring Memphis Red Sox's Neil Robinson, who had singled ahead of him, to register the first West squad run.

In the third inning, with two outs, Ted Jr. tripled to right center as New York Cuban right fielder Pancho Coimbre lost the drive in the sun. Unfortunately, Ted Jr.'s teammates were unable to advance him across home plate. The West squad scored its final two runs of the day in the eighth inning, as Ted Jr. used his speed and hustle to take advantage of errors by the East squad.[32]

The remainder of the game was anticlimactic. The East went on to defeat Ted Jr. and the West team 8–3. After the game, the South Side was abuzz with excitement and activities. Many of the nightspots and hotels in the Black Belt were filled with African Americans continuing the festivities of the 1941 All-Star Game. Unfortunately, the competitive juices flowed well after the game, and Ted Jr.'s teammate and manager was in the thick of the action as reported by the *Chicago Defender* on August 2, 1941.

Fight Follows East-West Classic

Newt Allen, shortstop and manager of the Kansas City Monarchs, and Jim Ford, second baseman of the St. Louis Stars, engaged in a fist-fight at the Vincennes Hotel following the East versus West baseball classic at Comiskey Park Sunday.

Allen was charged with two errors in the game before he was forced out when overcome by the heat. Ford supplanted Tommy Sampson of Birmingham at second base.

When the two players got to the Vincennes Hotel, Ford is said to have blamed Allen for causing the defeat of the West team. The East won 8 to 3 staging a six run rally off Double Duty Radcliffe in the visitor's fourth frame, the inning in which Buck Leonard of the Homestead Grays slapped out his home run.

Allen resented the accusation and hot words passed. The two men went to it but were separated by other players.

President J. B. Martin, of the Negro American league of which both clubs to which the two players are now under contract, acted promptly on Monday afternoon after getting the evidence of the fight.

Allen and Ford were fined $25 each and both men were suspended from playing with their teams for two weeks.[33]

6

THE FIFTEENTH SEASON

The Kansas City Monarchs were ending the 1941 Negro Leagues baseball season working to stay near or at the top of the league. Games against the rival Newark Eagles of Newark, New Jersey, in Yankee Stadium were on the docket, and articles in African American newspapers pumped on the scheduled matches with comments such as:

> With Johnny O'Neil at first, Rainey Bibbs at second, Jesse Williams in the short field and "Newt" Allen at the hot corner, the same infield that had the fans standing on their seats on their initial appearance here last month backed by their slugging outfield trio of Ted Strong in left, Willard Brown home run king, in center, and Willie Sims in right, the western kings of swat will enter the stadium to maintain their unblemished record.
>
> Strong and Brown are the leading extra base hitters of their circuit. Brown, himself, established the phenomenal record this year in a game at Kansas City of hitting four home runs in four successive times at bat. "Big Joe" Greene, who was the hitting star of their last appearance and the veteran Frank Duncan will take care of the catching assignments.[1]

One can only assume that the Monarchs would have taken the league title again, but we will never know. No records exist of league standings for 1941 and 1942. Ted Jr. continued his torrid pace of switching gears from one sport to the other. He was considered one of the best in both sports, and he prepared for another season with the Globetrotters.

In fourteen seasons, the Globetrotters won 2,022 games of 2,164 played in addition to capturing the world's professional championship. They were among the elite basketball teams in the country. They felt that the fifteenth season would be no different. However, before the first practice for the 1941–1942 season, the foundation of the Globetrotters' palace began to crack. The success of the all-African American Harlem Globetrotters didn't go unnoticed by other professional basketball leagues that had excluded African Americans from their teams. Success brought fans and with fans came money, especially if you could fill a stadium or gymnasium.

Allegedly, several veteran members of the Globetrotters, including Ted Jr., sought to form their own team. Even though Ted Jr. and other team members were at times better off than many African Americans before, during, and after the Great Depression, the monies were not enough to sustain them and their families. Ted Jr. liked the fine things in life—nice suits, shoes, and nightlife—that ate into his pocket regularly. Moreover, it appears that Saperstein charged team members for incidental expenses, such as bags and laundry services. For instance, Globetrotter payroll records obtained from the Abe Saperstein Archive Collection at the Dolph Briscoe Center for American History in Austin, Texas, show that Ted Jr.'s "basic rate" was $170 per month for the 1941–1942 basketball season. From December 1 to 15 he earned $94.05 with the addition of a $10 bonus and the deduction of $.95 for Social Security. In addition, "advances" to the players were commonplace. The payroll archives indicated that some players received advances that were deducted on payday.[2]

As the Globetrotter enterprise grew in stature and prestige, some of the players theorized that they could operate their own team and realize what Saperstein reportedly raked in financially. In the early years with the Globetrotters, Ted Jr. and some of the other players were caught in the excitement and stardom that came with the team's popularity. As they aged and more responsibilities developed, the paychecks didn't seem sufficient, especially when they heard younger players were receiving more money. The desire to enjoy life and not just survive—and to be entrepreneurial like Saperstein—made the players seek additional revenue. The effort to make more money would be overshadowed by a major event that would change the course of history for African Americans and the country as a whole.

Ted Jr. was among the players to join the squad for its first practice in November 1941 at the 184th Field Artillery Regiment Armory on Chicago's South Side. His good friends Bernie Price, Babe Pressley, Roosevelt Hudson, and Inman Jackson joined Ted Jr. on the floor for the first day's workout. All of them were veterans of a now world-famous Globetrotter organization that became the goal of many young African Americans longing to play for the heralded team. Owner Abe Saperstein wanted to challenge his veteran players. A number of new players reported for the workout, including one white player:

Reporting to owner Abe Saperstein and Manager Winfred S. Welch on Monday were the following: Charlie Young, guard from Atlantic City, N. J.; Tony Peyton, forward from Toledo, Ohio; Billy Jones, former University of Toledo forward and member of last year's Toledo White Huts quintet, a white organization; "Shanty" Barnett, East Liverpool, Ohio, forward, who played last year with South Carolina; Everett Marcell, Houston, Texas, forward from Southern University; Cleveland Bray, former Xavier University forward and all-Southern conference selection; Al Tacker, Dayton, Ohio and for three years forward on the Alabama State Teachers' college quintet, 7-foot George Atkins, former Oakland, Calif., high school center, and Ray Julian, former Wendell Phillips high school player.[3]

The team moved to Sheboygan, Wisconsin, where for fourteen days during the afternoon and evening, it scrimmaged against a professional league team, the Sheboygan Red Skins. When the season started, Ted Jr. and his veteran friends constituted the lineup. On Thanksgiving evening in Detroit the squad faced the Detroit Brown Bombers in the Brewster Recreation Center gymnasium. More than two thousand fans came out for the game. Ted Jr. played guard in this game and scored seven points while his friend Bernie Price played center and scored ten points.[4]

A little over a week later, the team was scheduled to play the Detroit Eagles at the Cincinnati Music Hall on Sunday night, December 7. The Globetrotters and the rest of America learned on the afternoon of December 7 that Japanese planes had attacked Pearl Harbor, destroyed the naval fleet, and inflicted a tremendous toll of American lives. Most Americans learned of the attack from the main media outlet of the day, the radio. President Franklin D. Roosevelt announced:

> On December 7, 1941—a date which will live in infamy—the United States of America was suddenly and deliberately attacked by naval and air forces of the Empire of Japan. Very many American lives have been lost. As Commander in Chief of the Army and Navy, I have directed that all measures be taken for our defense. Always will we remember the character of the onslaught against us.[5]

After destroying Pearl Harbor, Japan declared war on the United States and Great Britain, and the nation readied itself for Roosevelt's request to Congress to enter World War II.

While this frightening event was on the minds of most people, Ted Jr. and teammates still had a job to do. They played games in Cincinnati, Ohio; Decatur, Illinois; LaCrosse, Wisconsin; and Aberdeen, South Dakota. The squad traveled to DeKalb, Illinois, on December 10 and faced the current world titleholders, the Detroit Eagles, in a game played at DeKalb Teachers College, now known as Northern Illinois University. The newspaper report of the game in the *Chicago Defender* outlined the encounter this way:

> DE KALB, Ill.—(Special)—The original Harlem Globetrotters, 1940 world's professional basketball champions, gave every indication of having finally hit their best stride when they toyed with "Dutch" Dehnert's Detroit Eagles present world titleholders in a game played at De Kalb Teachers college here on December 10.
>
> The final score was 36 to 22 and might have been even more one-sided had not the Trotters eased up and proceeded to delight the crowd with their extensive repertoire of stunts and antics. The game was close for the first quarter, but from then on, with Roosey Hudson, the sharpshooting forward, finding the range, the Trotters began pulling away easily.
>
> Hudson had himself a field night with seven baskets and four free throws. Bernie Price, the great center, likewise was prominent, getting himself four of the Trotters' 16 field goals. Babe Pressley, Ted Strong, Bill Ford and Inman Jackson were brilliant on the defense as the Eagles were held to a scant eight baskets.
>
> The recent return of the veteran Bill Ford to the squad is one reason why the Trotters seem to have found themselves with a vengeance, and with Hudson again hitting the hoop with uncanny accuracy, it appears as if the wonder quintet is again the terror of old.[6]

The Globetrotters were like most Americans at that time, unsure of what the future held. They hoped that this new war effort would produce opportunities for African Americans. The following is how black Chicagoan Dempsey Travis reflected on this time:

> Three days after Pearl Harbor, Germany and Italy came to the aid of Japan and declared war on the United States. On December 19th, the Congress of the United States extended military conscription to include men between the ages of 20 to 44. Thousands of white men had begun to volunteer for service in the Air Corps, the Marines, the Navy, and the Army the day after Pearl Harbor. Black men were not permitted to volunteer for any duty except the Army and kitchen (mess) duty in the Navy.
>
> At the same time, American industry responded to the call by literally opening up thousands of new plants overnight. These factories ranged from huge shipbuilding yards employing masses of people, to tiny one-man operations in the basements of private homes. Many of the plants

in the union stockyards were on triple shifts. The magnates of industry and big business were recruiting Whites for the clean, new, high-paying war jobs, while the dirty, low-paying stockyard and steel mill jobs were being offered to Blacks. Low-paying or otherwise, there now existed a thirst for black laborers that had not been paralleled since World War I. And as white men and women left the cleaner jobs in the stockyards for positions in the defense industry, Blacks were pulled in as their replacements at Armour & Company, as well as other industries.[7]

Ted Jr. and the Globetrotters continued their winning games, but with each passing day, the war magnet pulled men and women into the call of duty. Despite the growing pull of the war effort, the Globetrotters prepared for the World Professional Basketball Tournament held from March 7 to 12 at the Chicago International Amphitheater. The team won its opening-round game defeating Hagerstown 40–33. Ted Jr. helped the team win its quarterfinal round game 37–32 over the Sheboygan Red Skins. However, the Globetrotters were unable to capture the crown in 1942. The team lost its semifinal round game 48–41 to the eventual 1942 champions, the Oshkosh All-Stars.

The Globetrotters played the tournament's third place game on March 11. Even though Ted Jr. led the scoring for his team with three field goals and five free throws despite sitting on the bench for most of the second half, the Globetrotters lost to the Long Island Grumman "V" Flyers 43–41.

Ted Jr. continued his solid play with the Globetrotters in the early portion of the 1942 season. Pictured with his hands extended in a spread-eagle stance, he is featured in the *Evening Times* newspaper in Cumberland, Maryland, on March 18 as the "Brilliant Cager" scheduled to face a Cumberland collegian team.

> Reputed to have the largest hands in basketball. Ted Strong, above, is one of the top stars of the Harlem Globe Trotter professional basketball team that comes here tonight to meet Coach Bill Keegan's Cumberland Collegians in the local team's final game of the season. Strong, who stands six-three and a half and weighs 210 pounds is playing his sixth season with the Harlemites.[8]

Ted Jr. honored his agreement with the Globetrotters until the start of the baseball season in April 1942. There was some doubt that Ted Jr. would play baseball with the Kansas City Monarchs. He knew his star still had altitude, and he negotiated for a better opportunity. In the April 25, 1942, edition of the *Chicago Defender*, Ted Jr. is shown in his Kansas City

Monarch uniform under the headline "Remains With Kansas City." The caption noted that Ted Jr. had an offer to play with an all-white Long Island, New York, team, but he spoke with the Monarch management and decided to sign for another year.[9]

Ted Jr. had to keep all options open, but he knew the Monarchs were the baseball team for him. He virtually grew up with most of the players on the team, and he could always find an extra payday with the great Satchel Paige. On Sunday afternoon, May 24, 1942, at Wrigley Field in Chicago, Ted Jr., Paige, and fellow Monarch teammates faced a white All-Stars team that included pitching sensations Bob Feller and Dizzy Dean. The press reported that thirty thousand fans witnessed the game. Ted Jr. played in right field as the Monarchs defeated Dean and company 3–1. By all accounts, the All-Stars were no match for the Monarchs. Most of the All-Stars were on furlough from the service. In fact, most of the white baseball league teams were depleted due to the drain of players signing up for the war.

As the months went on, it became apparent that the Kansas City Monarchs were the jewels of Negro baseball. They consistently outdrew most white baseball league teams in cities where they traveled. Ted Jr. and other Monarchs players reaped some benefits from this distinction. The Monarchs "were at the top of the Negro Leagues in terms of profitability and player salaries, which averaged $350 a month. Paige, of course, was in his own category of earnings."[10]

While the Monarchs were shining, the rest of Negro baseball didn't do too badly either. The public knew where to get their money's worth when attending a baseball game. *Chicago Defender* columnist Eddie Gant wrote in his column on June 27, 1942:

> Washington, D.C.—Negro baseball really came into its own here Thursday night. If there has ever been any doubts about the ability of the game, as it is played by colored teams, to draw, they certainly must have been dispelled under the brilliant arc lights at Griffith Stadium as 28,000 sat in raptured excitement as the Homestead Grays and the Kansas City Monarchs battled 10 innings.
>
> The Grays won the game, 2-1, with a brilliant, thrill-packed tenth inning rally after both teams had gone scoreless for nine innings, but that is a different story. We are more concerned with the people who paid to see the game and how much satisfaction they received in watching the Race players perform. Major league baseball in the white circuits has been unable to draw over 10,000 to their games, night or day, here

this season and when the Grays and Monarchs can pack 28,000 into the stadium then somebody is bound to pay attention.

When you closely analyze it, though, we would have been surprised if the teams did not draw that many fans. The Grays and Monarchs combined have some of the biggest names in Race baseball on their clubs—Satchel Paige, Josh Gibson, Buck Leonard, Hilton Smith, Ted Strong, Joe Greene, William Brown, Sammy Bankhead, Ray Brown, and we could continue to name them for another paragraph.

That game should wake up, not only the white league owners, who deny colored players an opportunity to play in the so-called major leagues, but should prick the ears of colored owners to the respect their own enterprise can gain if promoted properly. For years, the Monarchs and Grays, champions in the West and East, respectively, have been avoiding each other in a fall world series for the colored championship, but this Washington promotion should awaken them to what they have been missing by refusing to play each other. Why not a regularly arranged world series each year? This is the only way to properly determine the championship, and we are willing to bet that Race baseball will jump into the big money spotlight immediately.[11]

With the war effort heating up and more white players signing up to serve the country, white baseball league owners were feeling frustration at the box office. Attendance slacked, and the African American press exerted pressure to integrate all of baseball. The soul of the country was being lit by the talk of inclusion in sports and society in general.

Since the African American press continued its assault about the topic of racial inclusion in baseball, the Pittsburgh Pirates stepped up and requested Negro Leagues officials, sportswriters, managers, and owners to select four players from the East-West All-Star Game for tryouts. Ted Jr.'s name appeared with other Negro Leagues stars including Roy Campanella, Josh Gibson, Hilton Smith, Satchel Paige, Leon Day, and Bill Wright. The Pirates owners chose Josh Gibson, Willie Wells, Leon Day, and Sammy Bankhead and eight alternates, a list that included Ted Jr. Satchel Paige did not make the cut.

Wow, the opportunity they had been waiting for. Here was twenty-five-year-old Ted Jr. on a list of African American baseball players to be considered for a tryout on the all-white Pittsburgh Pirates baseball team. Now the waiting game began. The players still had a season to complete.

The Monarchs were the standout of the Negro Leagues. As the team approached the annual East-West All-Star Game, six of the top vote getters for the West squad were Kansas City Monarch players. When the final vote totals were published, Ted Jr. finished second in the tally for outfielders with 120,997 votes behind teammate Willard Brown, who received 133,572.

Ted Jr. shone as a star among the Stars. He regularly received lines of copy and photographs in articles and columns throughout the country during the 1942 baseball and basketball seasons. In the August 15, 1942, national edition of the *Chicago Defender,* he is pictured as part of the full-page coverage of the next day All-Star game under the headline "Dangerous At Bat."

The tenth annual East-West All-Star Game kicked off before a crowd of forty-eight thousand on the South Side of Chicago at Comiskey Park on Sunday, August 16. This year the Negro Leagues owners again decided to hold two All-Star games. The second game was slated for August 22 in Cleveland.

In front of his hometown fans and thousands of others who came from out of town to witness the annual event, the pitchers of the East team stumped Ted Jr. and his batting mates. Ted Jr. batted three times and managed one hit in a 5–2 defeat. Ted Jr. didn't fare well in the field as he lost a fly ball in the sun that allowed an untimely hit for the East squad.

Despite the sub-par performance in Chicago, Ted Jr. rebounded in the game in Cleveland, though the West All-Stars fell to the East 9–2 before a dismal crowd of only 10,791. This showing would be Ted Jr.'s final All-Star appearance. Fate had other plans.

7

1942–1943: A SEASON OF CHANGE, WORLD WAR II CALLS

While Strong Sr. and his wife, Vera, were busy raising the other members of their family, their nationally known firstborn son was the talk of the house and neighborhood. The family's two eldest children at the time, son Nathaniel and daughter Ollie, were twenty and seventeen years old respectively. Next in line was sixteen-year-old Othello, who was perfecting the pitching skills he learned from his father. In addition to the older children, Strong Sr. and his wife provided guidance to fourteen-year-old twins, Charlotte and Gwendolyn; Dorothy, twelve; Jasper, eight; and Tyrone, four.

When Ted Jr. got a chance, he would stop in to visit with his mother and father and younger siblings. Strong Sr. was forty-eight years old, and even he had to complete a draft registration card, which he did. The card documented that the family lived at 4819 Langley Avenue and that Strong Sr. was a minister at the Berean Baptist Church in Chicago. Strong Sr. was also busy running his community organization, the Afro National Economic League, which acquired properties throughout the Black Belt on Chicago's South Side.

Strong, Sr. exposed his children to community events, taking them to Ted Jr.'s baseball or basketball games in Chicago. Jasper Strong recalls vividly how he would go with his brother Othello to meet the Globetrotters bus as it pulled up to the team's hotel, and the players would disembark and check in before the next game.

"Yes, I would take the bags into the hotel, and Mr. Saperstein would give me ten dollars. Man, that was a lot of money back in those days," he reflected. "Mr. Saperstein also got me into some trouble. When I would get home and show my mother the money I had, she would take it saying that I shouldn't be walking around with that much money."[1] Jasper was delighted to just be a part of the spectacle that was the Globetrotters. The kids were proud of their older brother, and anytime they could be around the players, life was good.

At school and on the sandlots in their neighborhood, Ted Jr.'s younger siblings could brag about their older brother. They read the *Chicago Defender* newspaper and saw how he was a major part of the Kansas City Monarchs championship run. The August 29 edition of the *Defender* headlines reported that Ted Jr. helped his team battle the Chicago American Giants when he cracked the game-tying home run with a runner on base. The game went into extra innings after Ted Jr.'s homer, and the Monarchs defeated the Giants 4–3 in a game played in Kansas City, Missouri.

Ted Jr. and teammate Willard Brown hit home runs during a game at Comiskey Park on August 30, leading a barrage of hits by the Monarchs as they outslugged the Philadelphia Stars of the Negro National League 10–5 during interleague play. For the fourth year in a row, the Monarchs were crowned the champions of the Negro American League. They learned that the Homestead Grays would be their opponents in the 1942 Negro Leagues World Series.

The African American press promoted the series heavily since the two teams contained players who were household names in the African American community. Satchel Paige of the Monarchs and power-hitting Josh Gibson got most of the press, but African American baseball fans knew of Ted Jr., Hilton Smith, Willard Brown, and Roy Partlow, the Grays southpaw ace who threw a no-hit, no-run game on August 30 against the Chicago American Giants at Comiskey Park.

Remarkably, the Monarchs entered the series contest as underdogs since the Grays had defeated them in all four games they played during the regular season. In the first Colored World Series since 1927, the Monarchs knew the regular season meant nothing when it came to playing for the championship. They had great confidence in their lineup of left fielder Willie Simms, leading off; third baseman Newt Allen hitting second; third baseman Herb Cyrus in the third spot; right fielder Ted Jr. hitting cleanup; center fielder Willard Brown batting fifth; catcher Joe Greene in the six spot; first baseman Buck O'Neil in the seventh spot; and second baseman Bonnie Serrell in the eighth position. To complement the lineup, pitchers such as Hilton Smith and Satchel Paige could hit in the clutch.

This World Series event would be seen by many of the fan faithful in various cities. The games were played in New York, Chicago, Kansas City, and Washington, D.C., in addition to various exhibition games to give baseball fans a chance to see the teams play. In the first game played in Griffith Stadium in Washington, D.C., on Tuesday, September 8, the Monarchs blanked the Grays 8–0. Satchel Paige and Grays pitcher Roy Welmaker were marvelous for the first five innings, holding the teams scoreless. In the sixth inning, the Monarchs scored an unearned run as Ted Jr. smacked a single that sent teammate Newt Allen to second. While it appeared that a double play would materialize, fate had other plans and a series of fumbled catch attempts saw Ted Jr. attempting to score only to be tagged out at home plate. In the ninth inning, Ted Jr. again singled and then scored on a triple to deep center field by Willard Brown.

In the second game, played at Forbes Field in Pittsburgh, pitching again dominated for a good portion of the game with the Monarchs sprinkling a run in the first and fourth innings. In the first inning, Ted Jr. singled with two out and was advanced to second when Willard Brown walked. He scored when Joe Greene smacked a single. In the eighth inning, Ted Jr. was one of three Monarchs who singled, and they all scored when Bonnie Serrell tripled to deep center field. The Grays finally scored in the latter half of the game but to no avail as the Monarchs won 8–4. This is the game where the folklore of master pitcher Satchel Paige and master hitter Josh Gibson supposedly came to a head. Ted Jr. and his other teammates could only watch as this head-to-head matchup unfolded.

Author Donald Spivey, in his book *If You Were Only White: The Life of Leroy "Satchel" Paige*, describes what he learned about the faceoff from the pitcher. Paige was known as one of the master trash talkers in Negro Leagues baseball. A slight rain had developed and the crowd had somewhat diminished, but that didn't stop Paige from wanting to pit himself against the most superior home run hitter in all of baseball. Paige signaled his buddy Buck O'Neil to the mound and told him what he wanted to do. O'Neil signaled for Monarch manager Frank Duncan, who came to the mound and listened to Paige's plan. Duncan finally acquiesced and Paige walked two Grays batters to get to Gibson. Now, the truth would be revealed. What is best: superior pitching or superior hitting?

The ballpark crowd became silent as Gibson settled into the batter's box. The trash talking by Paige was complemented by Gibson, who gave it back as well as he took it. In the end, Ted Jr., his teammates, and the fans witnessed Paige strike out Gibson on three pitches. As Ted Jr. and teammates jogged back to the dugout, they passed Paige who strolled leisurely from the field. What a memory for the twenty-eight-year-old Ted Jr. to tell his friends and family members. The Series, however, was not over.

Game 3 saw the two teams squaring off in a night game at Yankee Stadium on Sunday, September 13. More than twenty-five thousand fans attended with New York City mayor Fiorello LaGuardia throwing out the ceremonial first pitch. This time the Grays grabbed a 2–0 lead in the first inning. That only lasted to the third inning. With two Monarch players aboard, Ted Jr. launched a home run into the right field stands, and Willard Brown followed with a home run in almost exactly the same location to make the score 4–2. The final score was 9–3.

The officially sanctioned fourth game of the Series was held at Shibe Park in Philadelphia on Sunday, September 29. A prior game held on Sunday, September 20, at Ruppert Stadium in Kansas City, Missouri, was disallowed after the Monarchs protested due to the Grays' use of ineligible players. Again, the Monarchs fell behind early, but Satchel Paige relieved starter Jack Matchett and held the Grays scoreless from the fourth inning on. In the fourth inning, Ted Jr. was hit by a pitch. He scored after Joe Greene sent a shot into the left field stands, bringing the score to 5–4 Grays. After taking the lead in the seventh, the Monarchs sealed the Series in the eighth with three more runs that involved Ted Jr. singling with one out and stealing second base. After Joe Greene walked, he and Ted Jr. scored on a triple by Buck O'Neil, who later crossed home plate when Bonnie Serrell doubled, making the score 9–5. The game ended with Satchel Paige striking out the last seven Homestead Grays. For the third year in a row, the Monarchs were champions, and they were the first Colored World Series champs since 1927.

For the Series, the switch-hitting Ted Jr. had a batting average of .316, an on-base percentage of .381, and a slugging percentage of .526. He was truly a key element of Black America's baseball team—the Kansas City Monarchs.

With the conclusion of the 1942 baseball season, Ted Jr. and teammates basked in the fame of being champions of the Negro Leagues baseball world. They also were anticipating the announcement of possible tryouts from the Pittsburgh Pirates. People white and black knew that the Kansas City Monarchs were a superb team filled with extraordinary players who would flourish in the white leagues where the salaries were bigger and the playing conditions top-notch.

Hopes were dashed as the *Defender* headline screamed across its sports page:

Baseball Season Over; No Big League Tryouts
Run-Around Given Negro Ball Players

The last two paragraphs of the story summed up the injustice:

> The day will come when Negroes may get a tryout in the major leagues. We didn't go into any conniption fit about it this year because the "applesauce" being dished out was sour.
>
> We want it done but we know it isn't done at the end of the season. Tryouts are given in the spring—and the teams train below the Mason and Dixie Line. More, too, we continue to pour our money into the box offices without any return. The owners believe we are satisfied. Hurt their pocketbook by staying away as long as the Negro ball player is kept out of the game and maybe we'll get somewhere. I said maybe. This is America and despite the fact we are engaged in a war of freedom of all people the color line or racial lines when it affects a Negro, has never been erased.[2]

Ted Jr. and other African American baseball players could only wonder in disbelief at the bitter hatred they endured from their fellow Americans. They knew they were good. They showed it season after season, even against the white players who constantly received top billing as "major leaguers." While this snubbing of African Americans was discussed in the press and the barbershops and hair salons in African American communities across the country, Ted Jr. and other Negro Leagues players needed to make money to eat and sleep.

The baseball season ended and basketball camps were about to open, but another event consistently preoccupied everyone's mind: World War II. Opportunities for African Americans were proliferating with defense plants ramping up and struggling to hire anyone who was able-bodied and willing to work. Shortly after the basketball camps opened, Ted Jr. played pick-up games with his buddies at the Studebaker defense plant on Chicago's South Side and took advantage of the golden opportunity to earn more money. His buddies knew he could play, and he had name recognition. It has been rumored that Ted Jr. didn't play with the Studebakers for the 1942–1943 season. However, data shows that he played ten regular-season games with the Studebakers. In fact, box scores that appeared in the *Chicago Defender* about the Studebakers' elimination in the National Professional League playoffs and the team's first-round lost in the World Professional Cage Championships identified Ted Jr. playing forward in the playoff game and at the guard position in the world championships.

Again, Ted Jr. was a participant in a history-making event. He played on the integrated Studebakers basketball team with white players Mike Novak, Jack Tierney, Paul Sokody, and Johnny Orr long before Nat "Sweetwater" Clifton in 1950 became the first African American player to sign a National Basketball Association contract. Even though the Studebakers just lasted one season, the team proved that integrated teams could exist if only given the chance.

The Studebakers were only four seconds away from advancing in the first round of the National Professional Basketball League tournament. But according to published reports, the "goat" for losing the game was Ted Jr. There wasn't much love lost for Ted Jr., and the African American writers had long memories of days gone by.

The *Chicago Defender*, March 20, 1943, read:

Studebakers Out of Pro Cage Meet
Minneapolis Wins in Last 29 Seconds
Chicagoans Blow 4-Point Lead in
Final Minutes of Hectic Game
Ted Strong the Goat

The final score was 45 to 44 and the Studebakers have no one to blame but themselves. Poor handling from the bench proved costly. Rumors floated about the Armory between the halves and after the game that Ted Strong, the man who dropped the fly ball in right field in the 1942 East versus West game, was at the Rhumboogie cabaret at 4:30 Sunday morning.

Strong was goat, among other things. He failed to take a shot at the basket with less than three minutes left to play. He might have been rushed. We will let it go at that but when Zaros, a Minneapolis player, stole the ball right out of his hands under the Minneapolis basket and made a field goal which tied the score 42 all, things didn't look so hot for a team that had any idea of winning the championship.[3]

Everybody Goes When the Wagon Comes
By Ole Nosey

. . . checking reports that TED STRONG of the Studebakers was floy-floying at the Rhumboogie the night before the team was beaten by the Minneapolis Sparklers 45 to 44 . . .[4]

Through the Years . . . Past Present Future
By Fay Young

The Studebakers went out in the first round play. A ball club, rated as tops was without a "guiding spirit." The team functioned mechanically—and there are those who went without "coffee and" for several mornings because they put their money on the Chicago boys. What the Studebakers need to know would fill several columns of space. The biggest thing is that you can't train in the Brass Rail or the Rhumboogie nightspots.

The fans were disgusted with the club for "blowing" a seven point lead in the second half and a four point lead in the final period. But when the Dayton Bombers player stole the ball out of Ted Strong's hand and sank a field goal that put Minneapolis in the lead, all of the Studebaker followers wondered why Strong was down under the basket instead of being or getting the ball down the other end of the court. Then they remembered that Strong dropped an easy fly ball in right field in the 1942 East versus West baseball classic.[5]

While Ted Jr. played sporadically with the Studebakers, another opportunity provided a new endeavor that he could never imagine. Immediately after the war broke out, thousands of white men volunteered for service in the Air Corps, the marines, the navy, and the army. In early January 1942, Rear Admiral Ben Moreell, Chief of the Bureau of Yards and Docks (BUDOCKS), received authority to "activate, organize, and man a unique, very special organization that would support the navy and marines in remote locations and defend themselves if attacked—the Naval Construction Battalions."[6] This organization was established because in 1940 the Navy had begun a program of building bases on far-flung Pacific islands using civilian contractors. When the United States officially entered the war, the use of civilian labor had to be halted. Under international law, civilians were not permitted to resist an enemy military attack. If they did, they could be executed as guerrillas.

The first naval construction unit was deployed in January 1942. On March 5, the Navy created the motto *Construimus Batumius*, or "We Build, We Fight"; designed a logo, the Fighting Bee; and officially named all Construction Battalion personnel Seabees.

African American men were not permitted to volunteer for any branch of the service except the army and kitchen duty in the navy. African Americans could not tolerate this blatant discrimination, and the National Association for the Advancement of Colored People (NAACP) pressed President Franklin D. Roosevelt and Navy Secretary Frank Knox to accept African Americans for service other than stewards. After months of negotiations, African American aspirations prevailed. On April 7, 1942, the navy announced that it would accept African Americans for the general service, with open enlistment for mess men and the new branch of the navy called the Seabees.

The word from Washington, D.C., went out in July 1942, and the *Chicago Defender* and other African American newspapers blared headlines announcing the navy's desire for volunteers to serve as Seabees. Readers of the articles learned that men who volunteered for the Seabees were not required to "quit their civilian jobs immediately."[7] The range of volunteers included barbers, construction workers, draftsmen, photographers, electricians, truck drivers, steel workers, and welders.

Types of Specialists Needed

The list of specialists for which there are openings in the headquarters companies follows:

Baker, barber, boatswain, chainman, chauffeur, chief of party, clerk, ship's cook, construction worker, driver, draftsman, instrument-man, mail clerk, photographer, rodman, sailmaker, steward, storekeeper.

In the construction companies:

Blacksmith, bull dozer operator, carpenter, concrete worker, construction worker, crane operator, dredge deckhand, driller, electrician, engine operator, excavation foreman, dredge fireman, gas and Diesel repairman, labor foreman, launchman, dredge mate, mechanic, oiler, shovel operator, painter, pile-driver foreman, pipefitter and plumber; pipelayer, powderman, rigger, road machine operator, sheet metal worker, steel worker, telephone and switchboard man, truck driver, water tender, welder, and wharf builder.[8]

Even though Ted Jr. and his buddies were professional baseball and basketball players, the thought of receiving a steady paycheck and serving their country was tempting. They needed to know more, and the *Defender* and other African American newspapers gave it to them. In October another article told of the navy seeking men for Overseas Work Units. Approximately one thousand men were being recruited for foreign service in an all-Negro unit of fighting construction workers (Seabees). The pay for recruits ranged from $54 a month to $96 for men who qualified for specific skilled positions. The navy established an age limit from fifteen to fifty years.[9]

While Ted Jr. kept playing baseball and basketball, more articles appeared calling for more officers' cooks, officers' stewards, and mess attendants in the navy. These jobs appealed to many African Americans who, unlike Ted Jr., needed work and wanted to serve their country. On December 5, 1942, President Roosevelt signed an order banning voluntary enlistments. Selective service became the law of the land due to the urgency of the war effort.

Once again racism reared its ugly head. In the December 19, 1942, national edition, the *Chicago Defender* in its "What the People Say" letters to the editor section ran a letter from "A Colored Member of the Seabees."

Sailor Blasts Bias in Navy Seabees

This is to inform you of the conditions and obstacles of oppression that are confronting the Negro of Seabees battalion of the United States Naval Reserve; we are "supposed" to be the only solid colored battalion in the Navy. But there are a number of people in this battalion that are assumed to be "colored" but are whites.

We were equal to any of the previous battalions that ever were at Camp Allen, Virginia, a number of leading newspapers carried photographs of our parade held at Camp Allen, Norfolk, Virginia early in October of 1942. The people of the United States are led to believe that we colored sailors of the 34th U. S. Naval construction battalion are treated as men of the highest branch of service of the nation, but on the other hand, we are constantly humiliated by some of our highest officers by calling us "niggers;" one particular instance or case was that of an ensign (withholding name) who told a mate that he would rather be with the Japs than with these "niggers" of the 34th U. S. Naval Construction battalion.

Upon our arrival in Los Angeles, Calif., on Dec. 2, we stopped at the Santa Fe railroad station's café for dinner. Our commander of the 34th told the head waitress of the café that he didn't want to eat in the same café with the colored men of the 34th. She told him that he could eat elsewhere if he didn't think that the men who are expected to win the war were good enough to eat in the same place with him.

Since reaching Camp Rousseau, Oxnard, Calif., there is a wide-spread display of signs of segregation and jim-crowism shown in this camp. Some of the boys tore some of the signs down and subsequently were put in the "brig" for these tactics, and others are told that we will be called "niggers" and like it. If there is anything you can do about these conditions, we (34th) will fully appreciate generous consideration. If you see fit to do anything about this matter, please withhold using name.

A Colored Member of the Seabees[10]

Ted Jr. and other African American men hoping to join the armed forces in defense of their country had no idea that navy officials were having a difficult time accepting African American recruits. Before the Japanese bombing of Pearl Harbor, the navy was a white men's country club with African Americans "serving" as servants. The navy had a policy of exclusion and fought to keep African Americans out for as long as possible.[11] The African American press and organizations such as the NAACP were lobbying President Roosevelt to have the navy abolish the Jim Crow policies. *Chicago Defender* columnist Charley Cherokee blasted the navy and the government for the stall tactics.

Anchors Aweigh Off

Good old over-dressed Navy is still a gentleman-officer's heaven and a negro's hell. Presently there are 74,000 Negroes in Navy, 7,100 of them "Seabees" construction battalion members, and an undetermined number messmen, waiter-bootblack servants. Pay off, chum, is that Selective Service will in November start sending most Negro draftees to Navy instead of Army.

Out-numbered, out-maneuvered liberals in Navy have given up on attempt to have a few Negro civilians commissioned officers. Except for a couple of Negro medical student ensigns, and a Coast Guardsman or so, there are no Negro Navy Officers. The whole department is nervous over "problems" of coming graduation of several Negro V-12 college program students who will have to be commissioned ensigns, unless a good excuse is found.[12]

In front of the backdrop of all the racial tensions in the military and the criticism of his play in basketball and baseball, Ted Jr. enlisted on April 22, 1943. He was twenty-six years old and in the prime of his athletic career. He entered into active service on April 29, 1943, as an Apprentice Seaman ("Seaman: Performs ordinary deck duties in connection with the upkeep and operations of a ship. Stands watch as lookout, telephone talker, messenger, or similar duty. Member of a gun crew").[13]

Like a majority of African Americans inducted into the navy at that time, Ted Jr. was assigned to the Naval Training Station in Great Lakes, Illinois, where he was enrolled in the navy's construction training course. On August 14, 1943, he was transferred to the 100th United States Naval Construction Battalion for duty. Ted Jr. was now a navy Seabee. He set out to serve his country well. The navy had commissioned the battalion on July 1, 1943, at Camp Peary, Magruder, Virginia, and sent them to Gulfport and Port Hueneme, California, before shipping the unit overseas on November 21, 1943.

Before shipping overseas, Ted Jr. did his best to make sure his wife, Ruth, had what she needed. He knew he could rely on his family to pitch in when required since Ruth was not from Chicago. His induction papers listed his address as 4819 Langley; occupation as a professional baseball and basketball player; income of $200 per month; and education nine and one-half years elementary, three years of high school, and no vocational school, college, or university.

Ted Jr. would soon learn what the rigors and racism could do to a man. He and other African Americans heeded the navy's call for workers. They toiled and succeeded in the training stations only to realize that promotions were not in their futures. To make matters worse, the navy selected southern white men to command Seabee units. The boiling point for tempers was on the horizon and the widely publicized members of the navy's 34th Construction Battalion, just returning from twenty-one months' service in the South Pacific, went on a hunger strike from March 2 to 3, 1945, at Camp Rousseau, Port Hueneme, California. One thousand African American Seabees refused to eat after it was learned that white enlisted men who were brought into the battalion were promoted to chief petty officer ranks. The African American members of the 34th Construction Battalion felt that with their overseas experience they were more than qualified to fill the petty officer ranks. Even though they refused to eat, the men performed all scheduled duties in order to not be accused of mutiny.

In response to the hunger strike, the navy top brass relieved the commanding officer, his executive officer, and a quarter of the original officers and petty officers. "Their replacements were all screened for racial prejudices and southern men predominately avoided. The new commanding officer, a New Yorker, organized a training program for enlisted personnel to be rerated and ensured that qualified men receive the promotions unfairly denied them under the previous commander."[14]

Despite the injustices that he may have been experiencing, Ted Jr., like many other African American men and women, served admirably. His status as a well-known basketball and baseball star remained constant while serving in the South Pacific. Ted Jr. stayed connected to the sports he loved and the men who covered them for the African American press. The following is from a September 15, 1945, column by Fay Young who conveyed the thoughts of the "one and only TED STRONG."

Through the Years
By Fay Young
Ted Strong in South Pacific

He played many a fine game in the outfield for the Kansas City Monarchs—and he was in several East vs. West All Star classics. This winter Abe Saperstein, who owns the famous Harlem Globetrotters' basketball team would like to have him in the lineup. But he is "somewhere in the South Pacific" doing his bit for his country. We speak of none other than the one and only TED STRONG, outfielder on the diamond and center on the cage court.

This week Ted writes that, "he wants all to know that he is well and doing okay." Then he has some things to say which might interest everybody.

"Not so long ago, I thought," writes Strong, "that I was on the best team in the world but I was wrong. We did lose a few games here and there. But this team I'm on now can't be beat, taking all comers in stride, barring none. Without boasting this IS the greatest team in history. Double plays, and double steals, this team executes all of these and more with regularity. Soon we'll be coming home. . . . Our baseball is a rising institution. If it can pass through this crisis, there's clear sailing ahead so keep it flying. Give the kids a break."[15]

He received entitlements to wear the Asiatic-Pacific Campaign ribbon, the Seabee insignia, and the Philippine Liberation ribbon. Moreover, he participated in the capture and occupation of Majuro Atoll, Marshall Islands.

The records also indicated that in July 1945 he updated his beneficiary form since his wife returned to Kansas City, Missouri. The document lists two children, although there is no indication from Ted Jr.'s friends or family that he and Ruth had children.

Before Ted Jr. returned from the service, things were not working well on the home front for Strong Sr. Although Strong Sr. and Vera did their best to maintain a stable relationship for the children who remained in the household, they separated in 1944. They had nurtured the children to adulthood but the spark had died, and with an involved lifestyle that had Strong Sr. participating in many community efforts, the couple probably grew apart. The couple still made time for Thaddeus, Jasper, Tyrone, and Dorothy, and they exposed them to events and activities that occurred in Bronzeville, as the Black Belt of the South Side of Chicago was now known.

8

THE BROTHERS RETURN

On January 20, 1946, the United States Navy honorably discharged Ted Jr. at the personnel support center in Bremerton, Washington, just outside of downtown Seattle. One can only guess that it was a co-incidence that the Harlem Globetrotters returned to Seattle for a line-up of games at the Seattle Civic Auditorium on Sunday afternoon, January 27. Ted Jr. shook off the cobwebs of sports inactivity and played in the game. The Globetrotters had a succession of games scheduled in the state of Washington, and it had to be a good feeling for Ted Jr. to reconnect with his teammates. Even Ted Jr.'s good friend Bernie Price was back. He suffered a broken leg in an auto accident in the summer of 1945 and had been accompanying the team in a coaching capacity. The *Chicago Defender* in its national edition of January 26, 1946, wrote: "It was quite a reunion when Strong got together again with Price, Zack Clayton, Roosevelt Hudson, Duke Cumberland, Lorenzo Davis and his other cronies with the Trotters."[1]

Whether Ted Jr. played in all of the games in Washington State is unclear; however, he was hearing reports that white organized baseball was focusing on "younger" African American players to bring into its league. He had just celebrated his twenty-ninth birthday on January 2, and he knew he wasn't an "old man" by any measure. He knew he wasn't in the situation that fellow Negro Leagues slugger Josh Gibson had found himself. The press was trumpeting that the famed home run slugger was "just about through as a baseball player."[2] Columnist Fay Young reported in March 1946 that Gibson was confined to a "Puerto Rican hospital early this season suffering from what was said to be a 'break down.' . . . When he improved, he rejoined the San Juan club but again became the source of trouble. He missed his air trip back to the States because he became so intoxicated, the story goes, that he couldn't get to the airport. Now he is accused by the police of walking around San Juan nude."[3]

Personal indiscretions weren't always blared in the media regularly, although Ted Jr. knew that people quietly talked about his love of the nightlife. People raised their eyebrows when he had a few stiff drinks too many. But this was the 1940s, and a good social life was just part of the environment of the baseball and basketball worlds—white and black. He probably felt that he could hold his liquor, and he almost certainly believed that he would never get into the position in which the "great Josh Gibson" found himself. If the truth be told, Ted Jr. had started nipping at the rim of a shot glass early in his sports career. Hanging out with the guys was what the players did, and he learned it from some of the older players. He probably wanted to fit in, and American society during that time projected the image of a man with a cigarette and a drink in one hand and a woman on his arm. Ted Jr. was young and impressionable, and he was thrust into the limelight because of his size, skills, and naïveté. His Kansas City Monarch teammate Buck O'Neil saw Ted Jr. this way:

> Ted was the type of guy who, if I came down and met him in the hotel lobby and said, "Come on, Ted, let's go to church," he'd want to go. But somebody could beat me down there and say, "Let's go to this dive down the street and drink all night," and he'd be all for it. That was Ted—he'd blow either way.[4]

Now that he was back from the Pacific Rim, Ted Jr. focused somewhat on resharpening his basketball skills and getting into playing shape, knowing that baseball spring training was around the corner. At six-feet-four and 220 pounds, he had natural sports ability. He was the big man for his day, and since things came so naturally for him, he probably didn't put a lot of effort into getting into tip-top shape. He could muscle an opponent out of position for a rebound, snatch the ball out of the air with one hand, and fire a strike to a teammate sprinting down court to score a layup.

He began playing baseball at a very young age, and instincts would take over because he played so many positions. He could scoop up a shot in the hole at shortstop and fire it to first base. At first base, he would snatch the ball thrown to him out of the air with one hand. He had the ability and confidence to know that he could do things that came easy to him. To observers, his flamboyant play would be construed as unconventional.

Even though criticism from sports veterans and authorities could be harsh, the average fan could only marvel at his abilities. Ted Jr.'s friends and family would only smile when they read about their beloved Trotters beating some local athletic club quintet with ease. There were times when reading articles from newspapers other than an African American newspaper could make you cringe and wonder. Case in point was an article from the Coshocton, Ohio, *Tribune* on March 16, 1946. The newspaper reported how the Globetrotters romped over the local Athletic Club 56–37. The article would make Globetrotters reading the results of their work shake their heads in disbelief. The insensitivity of the writer describing them as animals playing before laughing spectators baffled sane individuals due to the fact that they were human beings with God-given talents.

Colored Stars Uncork
Funfest after Building
Up Big Last Half Lead

Give 'em a herd of elephants and those darkskin dandies from Harlem would make Ringling Bros. fold up their big top and call it a season.

The basketball Glove Girdlers last night put on their "trained seal and wild west act" to the merriment of 1000 popeyed spectators as they romped to a 56-37 decision over the local Athletic Club quintet at Central gym.

What the colored cutups did with an ordinary basketball was surely something that the late Doc Naismith never had in mind when he hung up the peach basket and let 'er flicker.

The Trotters, building up a 20-point lead in the third quarter, cut loose—the ball was faster than the eye as they put on their rapid-fire spot passing, made the leather take crazy bounces with trick English, manipulated the ball on their fingertips at arms length and made the sphere disappear between their legs. And then came the baseball act with ape-armed Ted Strong winding up and letting the ball literally hang on his fingertips.[5]

On the same page as the Globetrotters article, there appeared a short article regarding George Mikan's entry into the professional ranks. Although some of the Globetrotters probably never saw the article, news of Mikan's salary disseminated through the basketball grapevine would have made many eyes widen. Sixty thousand dollars paid to a rookie professional basketball player was unprecedented in 1946.[6]

The Globetrotters, Ted Jr., and Mikan had two years to go before they would meet. But first, Ted Jr. would again visit the Pacific Rim, this time in the capacity of a member of his beloved Globetrotters. Even though the National Pro Basketball Championships were on tap at Chicago Stadium in several months, Globetrotter owner Abe Saperstein truly wanted to make his team international. In conjunction with the *Standard Examiner* newspaper of Ogden, Utah, he arranged a two-week series of games in Hawaii against the top four teams in the Island basketball league and various teams on South Pacific Islands. Saperstein chose seven players, and from April 2 to 16, 1946, Ted Jr., Reese "Goose" Tatum, Babe Pressley, Zack Clayton, Tom Sealy, John Scott, and Sam Wheeler did not lose a game playing every afternoon or night during the tour.

The success of the tour prompted Saperstein and Al Warden, sports editor of the *Standard Examiner,* to host a farewell dinner for the team on Wednesday, April 18. Everyone was elated with the team's reception in the Hawaiian Islands. The Saperstein publicity machine handled the promotional publicity for newspapers and radio.[7]

The Hawaiian trip was the forerunner of what would become a staple of the Globetrotters' operation. Saperstein witnessed Hawaiian dancing girls receiving accolades, and he decided to incorporate his own form of half-time entertainment.[8] The Hawaiian venture was just a prelude to other opportunities to build international prominence for the team. Ted Jr. was among the few who had been with Saperstein from the beginning, since his father, Strong Sr., agreed to let Saperstein take control of the basketball troupe he had organized. Saperstein obviously favored Ted Jr. He had his publicity team use Ted Jr. in photographs marketing the team, and Ted Jr. had remained loyal.

But Ted Jr. was freshly back from military service, and while he enjoyed touring with the Globetrotters, he had his other sport's passion to fulfill. He arrived back in the States just in time to rejoin the Kansas City Monarchs in Chicago for a doubleheader against the Chicago American Giants in Comiskey Park on a Sunday afternoon, May 5, at 1:30 p.m.

While Ted Jr. was away, a new black baseball league called the United States League was formed in 1945 by Brooklyn Dodgers president Branch Rickey and the East-West All-Star Game originator Gus Greenlee. A Cleveland attorney, John G. Shackelford, was named president of the new league based on his experience as a former player with several Negro Leagues teams in the 1920s. Greenlee was named vice president.

Greenlee revamped his Pittsburgh Crawfords and formed the league with teams such as the Toledo Cubs, the Brooklyn Brown Dodgers, the Chicago Brown Bombers, the Detroit Motor City Giants, and the Philadelphia Hilldales. Rickey's idea for this new league encompassed his belief that the white baseball leagues would accept an all-black league owned by a white American over an all-black league with African American ownership. Rickey unmercifully claimed that the Negro Leagues were in the zone of a racket, but, as many in the African American community knew, the Negro Leagues were as good or better than the white league—just not recognized.[9]

Despite all the fanfare, this league never played a game. And probably after this failed effort, Branch Rickey took the advice of African American sportswriter Wendell Smith and began looking at Jackie Robinson. Not everyone would have agreed with Smith about Robinson. Other African American sportswriters suggested the big names in Negro Leagues baseball. Many Negro Leagues players had their own thoughts:

> I won't say he was the best ballplayer we had in those days but he [Jackie Robinson] was adequate and we were all proud of him. Monte Irvin, Willie Wells, Ted Strong—they were all better than Jackie. —Ted "Double Duty" Radcliffe[10]

> We always thought that Ted Strong was about the most ideal ballplayer. Had all the tools. A switch hitter and could play just about anywhere. Anywhere you put Ted, Ted was at home—first base, shortstop, outfield. From outfield he could really throw; you couldn't take a turn from first to third on him. —Othello Renfroe[11]

Players were returning from active duty to the Monarchs. The team lost its young shortstop, Jackie Robinson, who had joined the Brooklyn Dodgers' Montreal Royals farm team. Monarch manager Frank Duncan chose Othello Renfroe to replace Robinson at shortstop. Ted Jr.'s longtime buddy, Willard Brown, who returned from the army, filled in at third base. Ted Jr., Johnni Scott, and Ford Smith made up the outfield for the Monarchs.

Ted Jr. was twenty-nine years old when he rejoined the Monarchs. The team still had its magic and winning form and finished the first half of the Negro American League season 27–8, ahead of the Birmingham Black Barons at 22–15. By the end of August, the Monarchs clinched the second half by taking the twilight game of a doubleheader against the Indianapolis Clowns in front of fifteen thousand in Kansas City. In the Negro National League, the Newark Eagles, winners of the first and second halves, captured the championship. Even though he batted .290 for the season, Ted Jr. didn't make the roster for the 1946 East-West All-Star Game, but his presence—along with teammates first baseman Buck O'Neil, who batted .353; Willard Brown, who captured the home run crown and batted .338; and second baseman Scott Thompson, who batted .296—made them the odds-on favorite to defeat the Newark Eagles in the Negro Leagues World Series. This would not be an easy affair for the Monarchs. The Eagles had such stars as pitcher Leon Day, who had just hurled in the East–West classic, and Monte Irvin, who had led the Negro National league in batting with a .395 average, followed by Larry Doby with .348, Andrew Patterson at .337, Johnny Davis with .335, and Leonard Pearson with .332.

While the buildup of the 1946 Negro Leagues World Series was in full play, life continued to evolve for the Strongs. Othello Strong received his discharge from the army in August 1946. Ted Jr. did what any older brother would do and contacted Abe Saperstein about giving young Othello the opportunity to play with the Harlem Globetrotters baseball team. Othello made the team, and Ted Jr. reached out to his longtime friend Al Spearman about going to the Globetrotters.

"He tried to get me to play, but I said no," Spearman said. "I went back to high school and graduated in 1947."[12]

9

"LIFE FOR ME AIN'T BEEN NO CRYSTAL STAIR"[1]

Ted Jr. spent many days in Kansas City, Missouri, after he met, courted, and married twenty-eight-year-old Ruth H. Jackson on September 2, 1939. After he returned from the war and the western U.S. tour with the Globetrotters, he headed for Kansas City and re-engaged with the Monarchs. But the adage "Absence makes the heart grow fonder" did not apply in the case of Ted Jr. and Ruth. His absence began to take a toll on the relationship.

As the World Series rolled around, Ted Jr. focused on the task of beating the Newark Eagles. The first game of the Series was a night game attended by nearly twenty thousand people at the Polo Grounds in New York on Tuesday, September 17. By game time, the temperature had dipped to the mid-sixties after registering a high of 84 degrees. Earlier that day on the same field and in front of 10,530 people, the St. Louis Cardinals completed a sweep of National League rival New York Giants by a score of 10–2.

New York City also played host to the white baseball leagues' policy committee meeting, where the white athletes received every concession they requested, which included a minimum starting salary of $5,000 beginning with the 1947 baseball season.

Regardless of what was occurring in the white leagues, the Negro Leagues World Series saw the Monarchs open the big game with their ace Hilton Smith on the mound while the Eagles countered with Leon Day. Ted Jr. and his teammates were ready. Henry Thompson greeted the first pitch from Day with a single to right. Singles by Herb Souell and Ted Jr. sent Thompson home with the initial run of the series.

In the sixth inning Satchel Paige relieved Smith after he had walked Larry Doby, who stole second as Paige struck out Monty Irvin. The Eagles got their first and only run of the game when Johnny Davis singled to right. Paige pitched four innings, struck out eight, walked none, and allowed just four hits. He scored the winning run after being driven home by Herb Souell. The Monarchs captured the first game 2–1.

The second game was played in Newark on Thursday night, September 19, and ten thousand baseball fans witnessed two of the Negro Leagues's finest vie for the title. Notables such as world heavyweight boxing champion Joe Louis and his entourage attended the game as guests of Eagles' owners Mr. and Mrs. Abe Manley, sitting in box seats at the back of the Eagles' dugout. On the mid-sixties-degree fall evening, the Brown Bomber threw out the first pitch: "a silver one emblematic of the first colored world championship back in 1888 and won by the Cuban Giants of Trenton, N. J."[2]

During the pregame festivities, Ted Jr. and teammates expressed their congratulations to the Brown Bomber on his previous night first-round victory over heavyweight contender Tami Mauriello in New York at Yankee Stadium. The fifth first-round knockout of a challenger didn't come easy for Joe Louis as his challenger sent him stumbling into the ropes from a smashing overhand right cross. The reigning heavyweight champion regained his senses and ended the contest in front of 38,494 boxing fans at 2:09 of the first round.

After the pregame festivities were completed, Ted Jr. and his cohorts jumped out to a lead on the National League champions but couldn't hold it going into the seventh inning. The *Chicago Defender* reported that Newark mayor Vincent J. Murphy challenged the Eagles by offering $25 to the first Newark player to score and $25 to the first player to hit a home run. The future Hall of Fame legend Larry Doby cashed in on both ends of the deal by scoring in the third inning and smashing a four-hundred-foot home run in the sixth. Ted Jr. did what he could to stop the comeback. He made a strong throw to third in an attempt to nail Newark's left fielder Johnny Davis. Monarch third baseman Herb Souell bungled the throw, and it went through his legs. Newark scored six runs in the seventh. In three at bats, Ted Jr. scored a run and didn't have a hit. The final score was Newark 7, Kansas City 4. After the game, the two teams packed and left for Kansas City and Blues Stadium for the third game on Sunday afternoon, September 22. Returning to Kansas City had its good and bad points for Ted Jr., but his Monarchs were in familiar surroundings where they were the toast of the town.

In game 3, the Monarchs jumped on the Eagles starting pitcher in the first inning and never looked back. The team scored a run in the fourth, fifth, and sixth innings, and in the eighth Ted Jr. topped it off with a 380-foot drive over the right-field wall with a man on to put the game out of reach. The final score: Kansas City 15, Newark 5.

Sunday night, September 22, wasn't unlike any other evening after a Monarchs victory. The area around 8th and Vine sparked with entertainment activity. Ted Jr. and his Monarchs teammates grabbed some dinner and late-night libations. Living in the northern section of Kansas City allowed African Americans to enjoy their community and all that it had to offer. Jazz music, restaurants, nightclubs, and hotels were prevalent in the African American section of segregated Kansas City. National music artists such as Billie Holiday, Sarah Vaughan, Dizzy Gillespie, Count Basie, and Charlie Parker flocked to perform in the Midwestern city.

After enjoying the culture of their times, Ted Jr. and his teammates prepared for the fourth game of the series, knowing that they only needed to do what they had done most of the season: score runs. They accomplished it in the prior games of the series, but they knew they couldn't become overconfident.

Monday evening, September 23, saw a seventy-one-degree day drop into the low sixties. About 3,800 patrons turned out for the game at Blues Stadium to see if the Monarchs could take command of the Series. Little did the fans know that the Eagles had a young pitching sensation up their sleeve. His name was Rufus Lewis, a rookie who had won nine games and lost one during the season. With his commanding pitches and his Eagle teammates scoring four runs before the fifth inning, the rookie resembled a young Satchel Paige, mowing down his opposition.[3]

The final score: Eagles 8, Monarchs 1.

The Monarchs had experienced this sort of letdown before during the 1946 season, so they weren't concerned about the lack of hitting output. They returned to their locker room to pack and head for the bus for the trip to Chicago for the fifth game of the Series. Their ace, Hilton Smith, veteran right-hander, was due to face the Eagles. The team felt good about its prospects to win the fifth game.

On Wednesday, September 25, the high temperature in Chicago hovered around seventy degrees, a beautiful day for a 2:20 p.m. game time start, although the low temperature for the day would be in the forties. The Comiskey Park turnstiles registered four thousand patrons for game 5. The Monarchs grabbed the lead in the fourth inning when twenty-seven-year-old Ford Smith, who was playing in right field in the place of Ted Jr., singled to center field, scoring Henry Thompson, who had walked and stolen second. The Monarchs pushed across two additional runs in the home half of the sixth and seventh innings, making it a 5–0 game. Pitcher Hilton Smith, who finished fourth in runs allowed in the Negro American League in 1946 with 3.30, had an outstanding pitching performance. He held the Eagles to ten scattered hits, walked one batter, and contributed with his bat by singling to left field in the seventh inning. In the eighth inning, the Eagles scored their only run after getting their only extra base hit when first baseman Leonard Pearson doubled to center, scoring Monte Irvin, who had singled. The Monarchs were now in the commanding position with a three-games-to-two lead on the Eagles. The saving grace for the Eagles was that games 6 and 7 were to be played in Ruppert Stadium in Newark, New Jersey.

Friday evening, September 27, posted a game-time temperature in the low sixties as the Monarchs and the Eagles took the field. Monarch manager Frank Duncan had to insert young Ford Smith again in the lineup for Ted Jr., who it was rumored had left the team to play in the Puerto Rican Winter League. After his team had dominated the Negro National League with a 43–14 record, Manager Duncan knew his talent and he used the six-foot-one, two-hundred-pound Smith, who could draw walks and hit for good contact. The Monarchs sent left-hander Jim LaMarque to the mound to face the ace for the Eagles, Leon Day.

The Kansas City team jumped on the Eagles starter with five runs in the first inning. The hometown fans wondered if their beloved Eagles were headed for defeat. The Monarchs meant business, and it showed when the home-run-hitting Willard Brown cracked a three-run blast. Day didn't make it out of the first inning as he was relieved by Charlie Hooker.

The fans received a reprieve when the Eagles responded with a four-run barrage in their half of the inning. The Monarchs left-hander couldn't retire the first three men he faced, and as a result Eagle first baseman Lenny Pearson and catcher Leon Ruffin singled to score the four runs. The Eagles captured the lead for good in the second inning as future Hall of Famer Monte Irvin hit his second homer of the Series with a man on base. The *Chicago Defender* reported the results of the remainder of the game:

> In the Newark fourth, Irvin singled and Pearson banged out a 375-foot home run. The final Newark tally was on Irvin's second home run for the game. The Monarchs scored their last two runs on singles by Willard Brown and (Buck) O'Neil in the seventh.[4]

The Series was now tied at 3–3 with the momentum back in the Eagles' favor. Moreover, the Eagles were unaware of another plus as the Monarch players and Duncan learned after the 9–7 defeat. Manager Duncan had planned to start Satchel Paige in the seventh and deciding game. But he couldn't locate him. Some of the players figured that Satchel was just being Satchel and would show up since he figured that the game wouldn't start without the Negro Leagues's prime attraction. Another rumor that has circulated for decades regarding the location of Paige revolved around his desire to get the winter paycheck lined up. The rumor appeared to be a good one for most people, and they immediately assumed that because they also couldn't locate Ted Jr. and Willard Brown. One had to surmise that the Monarchs center and right fielder were following in Paige's footsteps.

One of the Monarchs players in particular, Buck O'Neil, just shrugged at the situation and knew that his manager would field the best they had remaining and challenge for the championship. He wrote in his book *I Was Right On Time*:

> We had to go with Ford Smith on the mound, which actually didn't upset us at all because Ford was a good pitcher and Satchel hadn't exactly been overpowering against the Eagles. We also had to go with Hilton and Joe Greene, usually our catcher, in the outfield instead of Willard and Ted. All great players, but there we were, trying to play the seventh game of the World Series without Satchel Paige and two other guys I think belong in the Hall of Fame.[5]

On a seventy-two-degree Sunday afternoon on September 27, seven thousand fans showed up to witness a depleted Monarchs team enter the seventh game of the 1946 Negro Leagues World Series at Ruppert Stadium. Twenty-seven-year-old Ford Smith received the call from Manager Duncan to pitch the deciding game for the Monarchs. The Eagles sent twenty-eight-year-old army veteran and Negro Leagues rookie from Jackson, Mississippi, Rufus Lewis to the mound.

With Ford Smith assigned to the pitching duties, Joe Greene was called upon to play right field in Ted Jr.'s absence. Greene had been out of the lineup due to an injury to his throwing hand during a game against the Indianapolis Clowns in August. The six-foot-one, two-hundred-pound Greene took on the right field assignment even though he had been the catcher for the Monarchs before the injury. In the Negro Leagues, a player had to be prepared to play a variety of positions due to injuries and other unforeseen circumstances, and the final game of this Negro Leagues World

Series presented a challenge that called for every available player to rise to the occasion.

The Monarchs failed to score in their half of the first inning as Rufus Lewis didn't show signs of having the jitters against the mighty team from Kansas City. In the Newark half of the inning, it appeared that Ford Smith might match the pitching success of his counterpart when he retired center fielder James Wilkes for the first out. The second batter, third baseman Pat Patterson, reached base on an error by the Monarchs second baseman Henry Thompson. Second baseman Larry Doby stepped into the batter's box and Smith walked him, sending Patterson to second. With two on base and one out, shortstop Monte Irvin sent a single to right field and Patterson scored the first run of the game. Smith settled down after that and retired first baseman Leonard Pearson and left fielder Johnny Davis to get out of the inning.

For the next five innings, both pitchers mastered the hitters, scattering hits here and there. In the sixth inning, the Monarchs used the long ball to tie the score when first baseman Buck O'Neil deposited a 348-foot home run in the left-field seats. With the score now tied, the Monarchs needed Smith to maintain his mastery of the Eagles hitters. It just wasn't meant to be. In the bottom half of the sixth inning, Smith walked both Doby and Irvin. Left fielder Johnny Davis drove a double to left field, bringing in Doby and Irvin.

In the top of the seventh, the Monarchs scratched across one run when Joe Greene singled and then stole second. Monarch pitcher Smith pushed Greene to third base by hitting a single. Second baseman Souell then hit a single, driving in Greene to score the Monarchs' second run of the game. Unfortunately, the Monarchs stranded Smith and Souell.

The Eagles were now six outs away from capturing the coveted World Series crown, but the Monarchs would not go down quietly. In the top of the ninth, they put two men on base with two outs. Second baseman Herb Souell, who batted .344 for the series, faced Rufus Lewis with the opportunity to tie the game. The Monarchs' season ended as Souell hit a pop fly to first baseman Pearson.

The Eagles and their fans rejoiced in the victory. The 1946 World Series was the first appearance in the Negro Leagues World Series for the Eagles, and it capped an outstanding campaign for the team as it captured both halves of the Negro National League season, posting a 47–16 record for the year. The Series would go down as one of the classics in the history of Negro Leagues baseball. Moreover, six of the players (Monte Irvin,

Larry Doby, Leon Day, Satchel Paige, Hilton Smith, and Willard Brown) and Eagles manager Biz Mackey would eventually be inducted into the National Baseball Hall of Fame.

The Monarchs, on the other hand, could only imagine what could have been. For a number of years, they had been "African Americans' Team," and to lose a series they probably could have won easily was hard for some people in the African American community to take.

However, the great Buck O'Neil, always the visionary, said it best:

> Actually, you could also say there was something symbolic about those three guys missing the game. At that point, even though the Negro leagues had had their best season—clearing two million dollars in profit for the first time that year—it was true that most guys had their sights set on other things than black baseball. Jackie Robinson had played well in the minors, and while everyone was thrilled that Jackie would be coming to the majors soon, this meant the Negro leagues weren't going to be as important as they had been.[6]

Now, what happened to Ted Jr. after the 5–1 victory in Chicago? Sometime during the post–locker room activities, Ted Jr. received visitors who were strangers to him. They sat with him and discussed the Series. What happened next was told by Ted Jr. during an interview with the sports editor of the *Kansas City Call*. The article appeared in the October 11, 1946, edition of the newspaper. No other Monarch teammate, Strong family members, or friends have admitted knowing anything about what Ted Jr. told the sports editor. And those who could possibly have had an inside track on what occurred are probably dead. The interview opened with the following headline and lead paragraph:

Monarch Player Quits Team;
Says He Got Mad When Offered $750 Bribe

Ted Strong, right fielder for the Kansas City Monarchs, deserted the Monarchs, said J. L. Wilkinson, co-owner of the team, this week. He simply walked out on his team when it was fighting to win the 1946 Negro World Series championship. He left without giving notice or explanation, Mr. Wilkinson said. And, because he left us without a regular right fielder to replace him, I am of the opinion we lost the championship to the Newark Eagles, said Mr. Wilkinson.

Strong did not go with the team to Chicago for the fifth game of the series. After playing the fourth game here, he started to board the bus bound for Chicago with the rest of the team, but after putting his luggage aboard, he evidently changed his mind. He is said to have summoned a taxi and left the stadium, leaving the Monarchs loading the bus at the Blues stadium.

With Strong out of the lineup, the Monarchs had no regular right fielder during the last three games of the series in Chicago and Newark, and Manager Frank Duncan was forced to use pitchers in that position and had to recall Joe Greene, who had been on the bench for several weeks with a broken thumb, to fill a position.[7]

Ted Jr. confessed to leaving the team. He knew it was wrong, but even the mild-mannered thirty-year-old, who was known among family members as a "gentle giant," had his breaking point. He told the sports editor that this incident was basically the final straw. He and the entire team had to endure many things that they felt professionals shouldn't experience. The sports editor understood the conditions, so he pressed Ted Jr. on specifics about what happened after the fifth game had concluded. Ted Jr. had to lay it out clearly, and he began by explaining that three African American men approached him in the locker room and began questioning him about the Series and whether or not the Monarchs could prevail and win another Negro Leagues World Series title.

The sharply dressed men looked like gamblers to Ted Jr. He couldn't understand why they were approaching him since other Monarch players such as Buck O'Neil, Hilton Smith, and even Satchel Paige were more versed on the Monarch chances. Ted Jr. just wanted to play baseball, but to make the conversation more enticing, the men produced $750 in cash and asked what Ted Jr. really thought of the Monarchs' chances. The sports editor listened carefully to discover what occurred next, and Ted Jr. didn't let him down.

"I told them I would have nothing to do with their scheme," he said, "and I threatened them if they approached me again. I don't know whether they had talked to other team members or not. But I got sore about their coming to me. And the more I thought about it, the madder I got. So by leaving time I was thoroughly disgusted and decided not to leave."[8]

Taking a deep breath and sighing, Ted Jr. said that he regretted leaving the team. He knew that his team needed him. They were a team that had overcome many obstacles during the season. Why he didn't approach his buddies to get their perspective, only he knows. But then there was another view of the situation. Several months prior to the interview, in Kansas City, Missouri, a judgment had been rendered in the divorce proceedings *Ruth H. Strong, Plaintiff vs. Theodore R. Strong Jr., Defendant* that ordered Ted Jr. to pay alimony in the sum of $1,400 dollars at a rate of $100 dollars payable on the twenty-first of each month with the first payment due on August 21 until the judgment was satisfied. In addition to the judgment, Ted Jr. had to pay the attorney fees for his soon-to-be ex-wife and the fees for his own attorney who represented him at the proceedings on Wednesday, August 21, 1946.

Ted Jr. had a nice sum of money to pay, and people in the underworld probably knew of this. Seven hundred and fifty dollars in a cash lump sum would have been hard to resist, especially when that amount could satisfy at least half of the judgment quickly. Whether the sports editor knew of this judgment is unknown. If he did, he didn't divulge anything in the article. Ted Jr. apologized for leaving the team and stated that he let things get the best of him. He added that maybe his personality was "just built that way," and he realized that even when he was in the navy, he would get upset with circumstances but he couldn't just leave.

The six-foot-four-inch right fielder had to let people know about the dissatisfactions that plagued him and his teammates at times during the season. Shoddy bus transportation, inadequate room accommodations, and playing when hurt were just some of the problems encountered. He told the sports editor that he knew that if the Monarchs' owners were aware of the unacceptable conditions, they would have rectified the problems. It was well known that the Monarch owners had done many favors for Ted Jr., which he appreciated.

"After our last series with the Clowns, I was suffering from a charley horse. I asked for two days off to rest up before the series. I was given only one day off. All these things provoked me. And when the men tried to buy me on the Chicago game, I just blew my top, I guess. But I'm sorry now that I didn't talk it over with someone. And I am sorry if my absence caused the Monarchs to lose the series. I wanted the Monarchs to win the championship."[9]

Ted Jr. let a lot of people down. His anger got the best of him. The information that the *Kansas City Call* sports editor didn't put into his article is that his Monarchs' teammates couldn't figure out what happened, but they speculated when asked by Fay Young of the *Chicago Defender*.

"Some of his [Ted Jr.] cronies said Ted was having family troubles again."[10] An account by Buck O'Neil in his book *I Was Right On Time* indicated that the Monarchs determinedly wanted to win the Series, and they just figured Ted Jr. would eventually reappear in the lineup. The Monarchs had other problems on top of not having Ted Jr., since the Monarchs' other hard-hitting slugger Willard Brown, along with Satchel Paige, were missing too and would have to be replaced by teammates playing out of their normal positions.

What really happened when Ted Jr. lost his cool and vanished will probably remain a mystery. No one other than Ted Jr. knew of the mysterious men who "looked like gamblers." Moreover, one can only assume that the divorce judgment was satisfied since there are no records of him serving time in jail for not paying the alimony.

Ted Jr. always had a fallback position: the Harlem Globetrotters. He rejoined the team for the 1946–1947 basketball season, and the Globetrotters paraded him in publicity about upcoming games against such teams as the Cumberland, Maryland Amvets; the LaLonde Realtors, whom the Trotters faced in the Palatine, Illinois, high school gymnasium; and various teams in Ogden, Utah. As Ted Jr. continued to shine and receive accolades in basketball, the African American press reported the results of the 1946 Negro Leagues baseball season. Buck O'Neil won the individual batting honors, and fellow Monarch players Willard Brown and James LaMarque won recognition for best outfielder and best earned run average of regular pitchers, respectively. The Monarch team topped the league in team batting with .285. And Ted Jr.—he won the home run crown.

Despite Ted Jr.'s personal hiccup, the Monarchs were still considered the best team there ever was by many African Americans, especially in Kansas City and Ted Jr.'s hometown of Chicago. "Mary Jo Weaver, Miss Monarch in 1940, asserted, 'I don't think there was a black person in Kansas City that would miss a game. The Monarchs had been a dominant team since their beginning, but from the late thirties on, they were a powerhouse.'"[11]

An early portrait of Theodore Relighn Strong Sr.
Jasper Strong family archives

February 3, 1980   Theodore Strong Sr.

August 2, 1919: South Siders gather under the eye of mounted city police and state militia in the wake of the most violent riot in Chicago's history. In seven days of racial fighting persons were killed, 537 injured, and more than 1,000 left homeless. The violence erupted after stone-throwing at the 29th Street beach resulted in the death of a 17-year-old black you

The 1919 Chicago riots were the worst in U.S. history. Ted Strong Sr. is captured in this photograph as he walked among the people milling about in Chicago's Black Belt community. In the 1980s as I visited with Strong Sr., I was reading an article that contained this photograph. When asked if he remembered the 1919 riots, Strong Sr. replied, "Sure do!" Then he pointed at the photograph and said, "That's me right there." *Chicago Tribune, February 3, 1980*

Theodore Relighn Strong Sr. in 1977 at the age
of eighty-three. *Sherman L. Jenkins*

Ted Strong Jr. (left) takes time to pose with Memphis Red Sox player Joe Henry. *NoirTech Research, Inc.*

Ted Strong Jr. displayed skills that made him a standout in the Negro Leagues. As a member of the Kansas City Monarchs, he played with Negro standouts such as Satchel Paige, Willard Brown, Buck O'Neil, and Hilton Smith. *National Baseball Hall of Fame Library, Cooperstown, New York*

Ted Strong Jr. (far left) joins fellow East-West All-Star teammates in congratulating the St. Louis Stars Dan Wilson (being hoisted) who hit the home run to win the 1939 classic as the West squad defeated the East 4–2. *National Baseball Hall of Fame Library, Cooperstown, New York*

Group portrait of the Original Harlem Globetrotters basketball team wearing uniform patches reading, "Chicago $15,000 World's Pro Cage Tourney." Front row from left: Ted Strong Jr., Tony Wilcox, Roosevelt Hudson, Bill Ford, William Jones; back row: Louis "Babe" Pressley, Bernie Price, and Everett Marcell. December 1941. *Charles "Teenie" Harris Archive,* © *Carnegie Museum of Art, Pittsburgh: Heinz Family Fund*

Ted Jr. prior to beginning his tour of duty with the U.S. Navy Seabees circa 1943.
Jasper Strong family archives

Ebony Magazine in April 1947 did a feature exposé on the Globetrotters, and as part of the story, photographs taken during a prior publicity photo session were used. Photograph on the top right shows Ted Strong Jr. demonstrating his back arm balancing feat, which was a typical Ted Jr. move. The center photograph shows Ted Jr. flipping the basketball over his shoulder to pivot man Bernie Price. The third photograph features Ted Jr. displaying the baseball comic routine that was used during Globetrotter games. *Wayne Miller estate, Mangum Photo and Johnson Publishing Company*

The 1946 Kansas City Monarchs, champions of the Negro American League, are captured in this publicity photograph. Considered by African Americans as their "New York Yankees," the Monarchs played the Newark Eagles in the 1946 Negro Leagues World Series only to lose in seven games. Ted Jr. is standing second from the left. See close-up of him in the inset photo. *National Baseball Hall of Fame Library, Cooperstown, New York*

Ted Strong Jr. and legendary Globetrotter Marcus Haynes during a photography publicity session circa late 1940s. *Hank Walker estate/The LIFE Images Collection/Getty Images. Photograph by Hank Walker*

Ted Strong Jr. striking his baseball pose in his Globetrotters uniform. Ted Jr. was among the many players the Globetrotters publicized to market the team to fans. In news releases promoting an upcoming Globetrotter game, the publicist would state that Ted Jr. had the largest hands in basketball.
Harlem Globetrotters

At the conclusion of World War II, Ted Jr. and the Globetrotters took their show on the road to Hawaii. Here they are pictured about to board the plane for the trip. Ted Jr. is pictured in the back row along with (left to right) John Scott, Marques Haynes, Ducky Moore, Inman Jackson, and Sam Wheeler. In the front row are Bernie Price (dark suit, center) and (left to right) Babe Pressley, Ermer Roberson, and Boid Buie. *Vincent Price Family Archives*

The wedding of Jasper and Hazel Strong in 1966 in Paducah, Kentucky. Top photo shows Othello Strong standing next to his younger brother Jasper, Hazel, and Jacqueline Strong, Othello's wife and bridesmaid. Bottom photo shows the wedding party with Othello Strong far right and his wife, Jacqueline, standing far left. *Jasper and Hazel Strong archives*

Eighty-one-year-old Jasper Strong is the second-youngest child of Theodore Strong Sr. and Vera Strong. He lives in Chicago with his wife, Hazel. *Sherman L. Jenkins*

The gravesite headstone of Othello L. Strong in Burr Oak Cemetery in Alsip, Illinois, a suburb of Chicago. The Society for American Baseball Research (SABR) Negro Leagues Grave Marker Project made the headstone possible in 2005. *Sherman L. Jenkins*

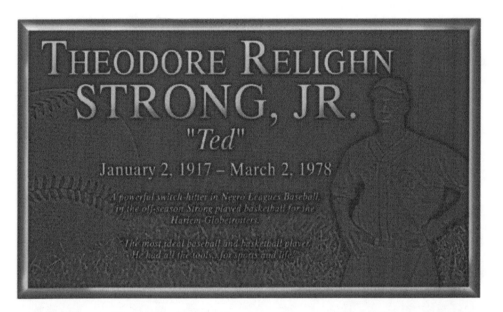

The mock-up (top) and actual grave headstone of Ted Jr. at Lincoln Cemetery in Blue Island, Illinois. The Society for American Baseball Research (SABR) Negro Leagues Grave Marker Project made the headstone possible in 2014. *Sherman L. Jenkins*

10

1947

Ted Jr. was riding the Globetrotters success to many places where Americans were enthusiastic about basketball entertainment. Whether it was Phoenix, Arizona, or Bismarck, North Dakota, he traveled and appeared in games where he was cheered for his basketball prowess and the antics that Abe Saperstein incorporated into the team's entertainment repertoire. The antics were part of the entertainment that helped distract white audiences in small-town America from the fact that their beloved all-white basketball teams were easily being trounced by the all-African American Globetrotter team.

On January 2, Ted Jr. celebrated his thirty-first birthday with teammates as they traveled to compete against local professional and semiprofessional basketball teams. As they celebrated, no one could have foretold that one of the Negro Leagues greatest home-run hitters would no longer be a drawing card. An Associated Press bulletin on January 21, 1947, announced that Josh Gibson had died of a stroke. The news was even more tragic since Gibson was only thirty-five years old. Many of the Negro Leagues players knew Gibson had been despondent about not being recognized for the talent he had displayed for so many years. With big Josh Gibson out of the picture and Jackie Robinson looming on the horizon, Negro Leagues baseball had some work to do, as discussed by *Chicago Defender* columnist Fay Young in February 1947:

> One trouble with Negro baseball is that the club owners do not make "name" players. The major league fans know the top players. A good example is Jackie Robinson of the Montreal Royals. Enough publicity has been ground out on Jackie to fill several books. If he makes the Brooklyn Dodgers this year or even next, white and Negro fans will

happily pay to see him in action as a big leaguer. They either have seen him play or have read enough to want to see him.

There was a time, some years ago, that we had some "name players" in Negro baseball. There was Andrew "Rube" Foster and all there need to be said was that "Foster is going to pitch today" and out came a great crowd to see the big fellow in action. Then there were John Henry Lloyd and Mendez, great shortstops; Cyclone Williams, pitcher; Oscar Charleston, first baseman, and Bullet Rogan, pitcher; Cristobel Torrienti, Cuban outfielder; Dick Lundy, infielder, and a dozen others.

In the last few years it has been Satchel Paige and Josh Gibson, who died a few weeks ago. Ol' Satch is still the magnet. It is about time we got busy and "played up" other ball players who are valuable both as players and drawing cards. Negro baseball has reached the stage where some added attraction must be put on to get the extra thousands out to the games.[1]

Life was happening. After Gibson's death, Ted Jr. decided that he had to live for today. "I told Ted that he had to keep himself clean because the scouts were probably still looking at him," Strong Sr. said. "Ted said, 'Ah, Dad, they are not going to pick us. I might as well enjoy life while I can.'"[2]

And so he did, in between basketball and baseball games, with increased regularity. Ted Jr. enjoyed the nightlife. Some of his basketball and baseball teammates assumed the same things about their vanishing opportunities to play in the "major" leagues. They knew their age would be a factor, and with Jim Crow in full swing and the example of broken past promises by white baseball team owners, having a good time became the norm.

Ted Jr. was about to test the international scope of "having a good time." After completing a basketball tour-team show in Cincinnati, Ohio, on February 22–23 that involved the Kansas City Stars, Hawaii Stars, and the House of David professional basketball teams, the Globetrotters boarded a private Pullman train car for Miami, Florida, and then caught a flight to Havana, Cuba, for the International Invitational Cup Tournament on February 25–27 in the Palacio de los Deportivos Hotel. The Globetrotters swept through the tournament undefeated.[3]

In a welcome break from Jim Crow America, the Cuban government treated the Globetrotters like royalty. Ted Jr. probably had a great time enjoying the tropical weather, hospitality, and famous Cuban nightlife offered by the pre-Castro hotels and resorts. After the victories in Cuba, the Globetrotters returned to America and picked up where they left off. On March 21 they traveled to Ogden, Utah, and took on Weber College for three games. Thereafter, the now celebrated Globetrotters flew to Honolulu for a series of sixteen games. The year before, the team had attracted nearly eighty thousand people in seventeen contests in the Hawaiian Islands. The life of a celebrated member of the Harlem Globetrotters always had its pluses and minuses. While they were touring the world, their salaries did not keep up. The team's expenses were covered, and they received a bonus here and there, but Ted Jr. and the other veteran Globetrotter teammates' salaries remained stagnant. With the fast pace of the team's schedule and expense coverage, Ted Jr. and some of the other veterans probably did not pay much attention to what they were putting into their pockets. They were getting something, and that was all that mattered.

On the baseball front, Ted Jr. and the Monarchs ownership agreed to let bygones be bygones regarding the 1946 World Series. The African American press reported that the Kansas City Monarchs were slated for another championship team. Ted Jr. was highlighted, along with Scott Brown, Buck O'Neil, and Herb Souell, as reasons the Monarchs' chances were good for 1947. The first home appearance of the 1947 season would be against the Chicago American Giants on May 4. But before the season could begin, one of the former Monarch players made national news that would change the face of professional baseball forever.

Robinson Plays Flawless Ball
With Brooklyn Dodgers Club

BROOKLYN, N. Y.—(Special)—Jackie Robinson, leading batter in the International League last year, was recalled from the Montreal Royals, league champions, by the Brooklyn Dodgers following the exhibition game at Ebbett's field on Thursday afternoon, April 10.

Robinson becomes the first Negro in about 55 years to play in major league baseball.

Thursday, in his farewell game with Montreal, Robinson played first base. He made no hits. He made seven putouts, no assists and no errors as his club whipped Brooklyn, 4 to 3.

It was during the middle of the game that Branch Rickey, president of the Brooklyn club, decided to bring Robinson up from the Class AA Montreal club, which is a farm team of the Dodgers.

Robinson went hitless in his first appearance as a Dodger on Friday when the Brooklyn team played and lost a 14 to 6 exhibition game to the New York Yankees.

Jackie popped up in the first with two out and two runs across. In the third, he flied out to left sending a run in after the catch. In the fifth, he reached first on a fielder's choice, one run scoring. Up the second time in that frame he flied out to center, another run scoring. He was up again in the seventh and was safe on Spud Chandler's error when Jackie laid down an intended infield sacrifice.

Robinson was credited with having batted in three runs. He handled 15 chances with an error at first base.[4]

The African American community reverberated with many "I told you so!" exclamations when the news hit the streets. The talk now that Robinson had made it centered on who would be next. With so many superb candidates, it wasn't a matter of whom but when. Speculation is that Ted Jr. held a flicker of hope, but he probably figured that if he was selected, he would be notified while he was enjoying himself in a fancy nightclub after a basketball or baseball game. Ted Jr. no doubt felt like his friend Buck O'Neil, who said:

> It was true that most guys had their sights set on other things than black baseball. Jackie Robinson had played well in the minors, and while everyone was thrilled that Jackie would be coming to the majors soon, this meant that Negro Leagues weren't going to be as important as they had been.[5]

That sentiment didn't deter the aspirations of young African Americans who still saw the Negro Leagues as their shot at playing professional baseball. After all, Jackie Robinson was a product of the African American baseball franchise.

Regardless of the external events going on around him, Ted Jr. continued his career with the Globetrotters and forged ahead in the 1947 baseball season. An article by *Defender* columnist Fay Young on August 2, 1947, dashed his hopes:

Skunks Stay Away

If the Negro player makes or players make good, they will have to be careful of their conduct both on and off the field. In other words, the major league owners and managers will stand for "no stuff" to be pulled. There is no place on any club for the foul-mouthed, uncouth, liquor drinking, huzzy-chasing player. To them he is a plain "rat" and won't get into the barrel to spoil the rest of the lot. This applies to white as well as Negro players.

The white owners prefer men under 26. Married, decent respectable and home loving citizens. If they don't measure up they won't break through even if they can hit like Babe Ruth or pitch like Buck Newsom or field like Joe DiMaggio.[6]

So much for Ted Jr. He would lend his knowledge of the game to his younger brother. However, for young African American boys looking forward to playing professional baseball, the signing of other Negro Leagues ball players shortly after the Robinson announcement only increased hopes and aspirations. The list of elite players impressed many fans:

- Larry Doby, Newark Eagles infielder, signed with the Cleveland Indians.
- Willard J. Brown and Henry Thompson, Kansas City Monarchs outfielder and infielder, signed with the St. Louis Browns.
- Roy Campanella, Baltimore Elite Giants, signed with the Dodgers.

These announcements of African Americans' transition to white teams only heightened anticipation of the annual East-West All-Star Game, scheduled for Sunday, July 27, at Comiskey Park in Chicago. For the fifth year in a row, the fans did not see fit to elect Ted Jr. to the West squad for the annual event. Even though he managed to become the home run king in 1946, his disappearance in the 1946 Negro Leagues World Series tainted his reputation. The excitement over Jackie Robinson and other Negro Leagues players signing contracts with white teams also overshadowed Ted Jr.'s accomplishments.

He played out the remainder of the 1947 season with the Monarchs. It would be his last year with a team that the African American community in the United States felt was its "Team." Ted Jr. was among the best there was in Negro Leagues baseball, and he was a bright example of excellence in basketball with the Harlem Globetrotters. However, a new crop of athletes, young, vibrant, and eager to show their stuff, were on the rise, and just having the "natural ability" wasn't going to cut it anymore. The discipline to train and to commit oneself to always be the best was becoming the norm. Wine, women, and song were slowly being replaced, but Ted Jr. wasn't ready to see it that way. As noted historian Tim Black put it, "Ted believed he could do any damn thing."[7] He wasn't from Missouri, but the inexorable evolution of professional sports was showing him that his days as an athlete were slowly coming to an end. The disappointing factor in the Ted Jr. saga was the fact that he had only known baseball and basketball. Professional sports could be good paying jobs for African Americans who were at Ted Jr.'s level. He probably relished the professional sports atmosphere, and with friends like Abe Saperstein, he figured he could depend on them to keep him afloat. As fate would attest, Ted Jr. still had a few good moments left.

The 1947–1948 basketball season for the Harlem Globetrotters opened in Chicago on Thursday, November 13, against the Carlisle Indians at Chicago Stadium. The following Thursday, November 20, the internationally known team took on the New York Celtics, the nationally known white professional basketball team. The *Chicago Defender* reported that the Globetrotters had signed Lorenzo "Piper" Davis, who had played baseball for the Birmingham Black Barons. This would be the seventh season that Davis had played with the Globetrotters. "Other veterans who will be back are Ermer Robinson, Marquis Haynes, Bernie Price, John Scott, Sam Wheeler, Ted Strong, and others."[8]

Abe Saperstein saw the prospects of his team reclaiming the prestige of old since the World War had ended and prosperity abounded in the United States. It would only be a matter of time before one of Saperstein's prime players, Reece "Goose" Tatum, would rejoin the team after his stint in the military. Saperstein began preparing for the game he felt basketball fans clamored to see and one that he felt would put the Harlem Globetrotters truly on top of the basketball world.

The National Professional Basketball League had been established and had drawn college stars such as George Mikan and leaping Jim Pollard, "who was even better than Mikan, some insisted,"[9] and others to its fold. George Mikan was a standout at DePaul in Chicago. He was six-foot-eleven and a mountain under the basket, and he generated tremendous news coverage from the white press. He joined the Minneapolis Lakers, a team that was "tearing up the National Basketball League (NBL) and being touted as the best basketball team ever."[10]

Saperstein took the game so seriously that "he merged the best players from his East and West Units to create what he felt was a powerhouse team."[11] Ted Jr. was a member of the "powerhouse" Globetrotter team. The Saperstein publicity machine began hammering on the claim that the Globetrotters had a 102-game winning streak going.

"However many consecutive victories it was, the mighty Lakers," the Chicago papers wrote, "may put the first blotch" on the Trotters' streak. As actors and performers, as tricksters, the Globetrotters were brilliant. But their play was all theater, not basketball. Goose Tatum was described as a "Negro pivot clown," who may have had arms so long Mikan would think he was confronting an octopus, but for the first time the Trotters would "have a basketball game on their hands."[12]

The Globetrotters' squad kept to a rigorous playing schedule that bordered on insanity. Newspapers pointed out that they had been on the road for five straight nights and speculated that they would be tired. However, the truth was that they played *every night,* night after night, and none of them could have counted how many straight nights they had been traveling. In just the month before this game, they had gone from Minnesota to South Dakota, down to Nebraska and Missouri, then out to California, on up to Washington, back down to New Mexico and Oklahoma, then they had worked their way north to Missouri, and finally the night before this game, they had played in Peoria, Illinois.[13]

The African American community was aware of the importance of this game. Many from the Black Belt in Chicago were among the 17,823 fans, spectators to witness the "Game of the Year." Members of the African American community were proud of the Globetrotters.

"Ted and his teammates were playing by their rules and beating the white teams," Black explained.[14] Then, Black put it another way: "Whether we were athletes or not, there was no point of feeling inferior. I can take your rules and beat you. I am not saying they are good rules but they are your rules and I have to abide by them."[15]

Ted Jr. and teammates knew they had family and friends in the crowd rooting for them. The game went back and forth until the half as the Lakers took the lead. The second half became one of the biggest thrills for the seventeen thousand plus basketball fans in attendance. The *Chicago Defender* reported:

Story Book Finish

It was a thrilling ending if there ever was one. No storybook game could have had any better finish. In the closing minutes, the Globetrotters were in front, 59-56. Jim Pollard came through with a basket, which moved the Lakers within one point of a tie, 59-58. Goose Tatum fouled Mikan and Mikan missed the free-gift shot. Tatum went out on five personal fouls, Wheeler of Detroit replacing him. Pressley was already out of the game on five personals, Ted Strong going into the lineup.

Wheeler fouled Mikan and the clock was stopped on the three-minute ruling which calls for the stoppage whenever the ball is dead. Mikan made good his free toss and the score was tied 59 all.

The seconds slicked off—45, 40, 30 and onto 3. The Globetrotters fans yelled, "freeze the ball." They preferred a 5-minute overtime game rather than allow the Lakers to get hold of the ball and make a long shot and win the game.

What an Ending

Then Robinson set himself and let go the ball. It was a desperate effort to win.

Up into the air went the ball.

"Bang" went the gun ending the game. But the ball was still in play.

Through the hoop it went. The crowd was in a frenzy. Up went the referee's arms denoting the field goal was good. He then rushed over to the scorers' table to notify them.

The Globetrotters rushed over and lifted Robinson on their shoulders. Owner-Coach Abe Saperstein headed the parade to the dressing room. His team, the greatest ever seen in the history of Windy City basketball, had done the seemingly impossible thing.[16]

Ted Jr. and his teammates "had done the seemingly impossible thing," and it placed pride on the mantel of many households in the Black Belt.

"They gave us the opportunity to go back to our neighborhood and brag about the guys we knew on the team," Tim Black said. "The cream of the crop. They played because they believed they were the cream of the crop. Ted believed he could do any damn thing. We saw all the time that he had that inner confidence."[17]

After pausing for a moment, Black added, "They were older but they were our contemporaries. What Ted and the others exemplified for us was overcoming the impossible. They had broken, in their time, the racial barrier, the quality of life barrier that others accused us of not having. They exemplified overcoming the impossible and making it possible on the court and beyond."[18]

Even though Ted Jr. only played in the last quarter of the historic game, that didn't seem to bother Black and other friends of the Strong family like Morris Gordon. But history doesn't always understand when viewed from a historian's vantage point. Author John Christgau in his book *Tricksters in the Madhouse* dedicated a chapter titled "Ted." Christgau's book is a play-by-play account of the historic game, and a reader thinks that one will learn of Ted Jr.'s play in the game, but you don't learn of Ted Jr.'s participation until the final two paragraphs of the chapter:

Ted Strong replaces Pressley. At six-five, 220 pounds, he is the one Globetrotter whose height and muscular frame seem to equip him to do battle against the taller Lakers. He has broad shoulders, a thick neck, huge hands, burly thighs that threaten to rip the piping of his stretched pants, and biceps that seem to have been inflated by tire pumps.

Strong is a twelve-year veteran of the Globetrotters, and by virtue of his experience and the authority of his size, he would seem to be the team's natural leader. But basketball is his second love, behind the pleasures of a stiff drink now and then and performing as a slugging outfielder for the Kansas City Monarchs in the Negro Leagues. Globetrotters' publicity pictures of him winding up with the basketball squeezed in his huge hand, one leg raised in the high kick of a flamethrowing pitcher, suggest where his real talent lives. But as he rumbles onto the floor and heads for his spot on the free throw-line, he cuts through the free-throw circle, where Mikan is waiting to be awarded the ball. As he passes slowly in the shadow of Mikan, who has popped his glasses and is cleaning them on his shirttail, Strong's powerful frame seems daunting, and the question is obvious: Where has he been?[19]

Ted Jr.'s. participation was minimal, but he was there because Abe Saperstein chose him to be a member of the squad. At thirty-one years of age and with twelve years of experience with the Globetrotters, Ted Jr. obviously still had something left in the tank even if it wasn't anything more than having the presence of a big squad to compete against the Lakers. The victory over the Lakers was monumental. Ted Jr. and teammates celebrated well into the wee hours of February 20. As a reward for the win, Abe Saperstein presented each player with a cash bonus. The amount of the bonus depends on with whom you talked. The amount ranged from $100 to $1,000. Either way it was a nice sum to receive back in 1948.

Unfortunately, Ted Jr.'s teammate Marques Haynes wasn't able to join the squad for the celebration in the Black Belt on the South Side at the Persian Hotel, where they were the guests of honor at a party. "Marques Haynes was in such pain from his two horrendous falls that he went back to the Trotters' rooming house and went to bed. The next morning, he could barely move and decided to go to the hospital, where X-rays confirmed that he fractured the fourth lumbar vertebra. Amazingly, he played the second half with a broken back. The doctors put him in a full body cast and he walked out of the hospital, but he was through for the season."[20]

This victory in Chicago did nothing to improve Ted Jr.'s personal life. Published reports beginning with his disappearance from the 1946 World Series to various league games throughout the 1947 baseball season focused on Ted Jr.'s "family problems." Since he didn't have any children, the "family problems" could only stem from the strained relationship he had with his ex-wife.

It could have been at any of the many parties Ted Jr. and his teammates visited after the Lakers game that he met a young twenty-one-year-old African American woman named Florence Faulkner. Their relationship moved quickly as 1948 evolved.

Basketball season and the victory over the Lakers soon became a fading memory. Baseball was on the horizon and money needed to be made. After the 1946 World Series incident, going back to the Monarchs wasn't going to be in the cards even though Ted Jr. explained why he left the team and many people believed him. In fact, no other sportswriter picked up on the story by the *Kansas City Call* sports editor. Although Ted Jr. didn't speak ill of the Monarchs ownership, feathers were ruffled. Ted had been a key element in the Monarchs' championship run.

Ted needed to land somewhere in the Negro Leagues, and on the eve of the opening of spring training in March 1948, the press announced that Ted Jr. and Reece "Goose" Tatum had signed with the Indianapolis Clowns of the Negro American League.[21] Ted Jr. and Tatum had become running buddies, and they evidently established themselves as a one-two punch for the Clowns. Tatum's showmanship and Ted Jr.'s hitting and fielding skills gave the team the spark it needed.

However, neither Tatum nor Ted Jr. could overcome the onslaught of the white leagues grabbing the stars of the Negro Leagues. Word had been circulating that the white leagues would soon tap ol' Satchel Paige. Ted Jr. probably had nothing but smiles for his old friend. Paige had been a big brother to Ted Jr., and he knew that the great Satchel Paige, even at forty-two years old in 1948, could still take on the best the white leagues could offer.

As opening day approached for the 1948 baseball season, Ted Jr. and Goose Tatum participated in the Clowns' spring training camp in New Orleans. A minor setback occurred when, in late April just weeks before the Clown's opener on May 2 in New Orleans, Tatum suffered acute appendicitis and was rushed to the hospital for emergency surgery in Dothan, Alabama. As the local doctors predicted, Tatum left the hospital and was back in uniform before the opener. The Clowns took the setback in stride and prepared to play a rigorous schedule. In Columbus, Ohio, in June 1948, Ted Jr. flashed images of his former self. Spectators at Red Bird Stadium witnessed Ted Jr. hit a towering drive 425 feet over the center-field fence.

Ted Jr. showed his former team that he still could hit mammoth home runs and perform like the Ted Jr. of old. While he fought to reestablish himself in Negro Leagues baseball, his younger brother Othello was receiving high marks for his play with the Globetrotters baseball team.

"Way to go, Ted and Othello!" was the cry from the Strong clan. The older brother was showing he still had it, and the younger sibling continued to impress.

The summer of 1948 looked even brighter when on July 5, 1948, Satchel Paige received a letter from Abe Saperstein asking him, "How soon can you be in Cleveland for a tryout with the Indians?"[22] After the mock tryout concluded, author Donald Spivey described what happened:

> The pressure was on Paige to deliver, and his first opportunity came in an exhibition game against the Brooklyn Dodgers at Cleveland Mu-

nicipal Stadium on July 15, 1948. It was not an accident that 64,877 fans showed up for an exhibition game on a Wednesday night. [Bill] Veeck and any of the other smart promoters knew that the large turn-out was because of the presence of Satchel Paige. And it was Paige who "gave the Cleveland fans their biggest thrill" that night. The crowd witnessed a "brilliant two-inning relief chore by Paige, ageless Negro hurler recently signed by the Tribe." Paige came in to take the mound in the seventh inning and threw a total of twelve pitches and struck out the side. He retired Gil Hodges with four pitches, took out Irvin Palica with three, and blasted Tommy Brown out with a combination of fancy curves and sonic fastballs. He then struck out three other would-be hitters in the eighth to conclude his magnificent strikeout performance for the night. The crowd went wild. Cleveland took the contest 4-3.[23]

That same evening at the Polo Grounds in New York, Ted Jr. and his new teammates clashed with the New York Cubans. The game included "the side-splitting side show antics of 'King Tut' and 'Juggling' Joe Taylor."[24]

As quickly as Ted Jr. and Goose Tatum joined the Indianapolis Clowns, they soon departed. Chances are they overstayed their welcome when they coupled their playing time with sampling the nightlife and having a good time. Indianapolis owner Syd Pollack had seen enough, and he suspended Ted Jr. for the balance of the season and put Tatum on "definite" suspension for missing games. When you look at the team's standings for the first and second halves of the season, the Clowns were a losing ballclub, and they finished the 1948 season next to last in the Negro American League standings.

This was a second major setback for Ted Jr. In the past, he had been able to rely on his extraordinary natural talent. However, with advancing age, years of cavorting, and now a buddy to join him in the libations and nightlife that were open to sports stars, he easily slipped from the good graces of his team's owner. The grapevine had already entangled the man from Chicago who had shown so much potential. People in various sports and social circles whispered, "What a waste. He was a very good athlete. There wasn't no telling how good he would have been if he'd have just played baseball and stayed away from that bottle."[25] In the midst of the whispers and snubs, Ted Jr. knew he could depend on his family to always greet him warmly and openly.

"Oh, when my father would have a cook-out, Ted and my other brothers and their families would come over and we would just have a ball," Jasper Strong said. "My brothers would play cards and drink a little and listen to music way into the night. It was just so much fun listening to them tell the sports stories and the other things they experienced."[26]

Strong Sr. and Vera were now living at 4819 Langley Avenue in Chicago with their seven children, including the soon-to-be-fourteen-year-old Jasper, who at age eighty is alive at the time of this writing. Jasper Strong recalled that his father always had a project going. The Afro National Economic League, begun in 1922 by Strong Sr., folded in 1948. The community organization was dedicated to working for better housing and jobs for African Americans on the South Side. Strong Sr. continued his work in the ministry, which he loved, and at one point he served as assistant minister at Berean Baptist Church.[27]

Most of America swirled in the rising prosperity of the postwar era, and some of that prosperity began to trickle down to African Americans in areas like the Black Belt of Chicago. African Americans were developing shopping districts, such as 47th Street and South Parkway (now King Drive), department stores, movie theaters, and hotels like the Pershing, which housed the famous Pershing Ballroom and "was the largest hotel of its type owned by blacks until the mid-1940s."[28] Mr. and Mrs. Strong kept a disciplined household, but word of mouth about the excitement of the nightlife intrigued the older Strong children. Some of the best African American rhythm and blues musicians held court in some of the finest spots in the Black Belt. In 1948 Aristocrat Records (later to become the famed Chess Records) "broke new ground and set the tone for rhythm and blues for the next 10 years with the release of Muddy Waters' 'I Can't Be Satisfied.'"[29] This wave of activity was fueled when on May 4 the U.S. Supreme Court outlawed private agreements, forbidding ownership of real estate to people of a designated race or color. In two 6 to 3 decisions, the Supreme Court ruled that the agreements, known at the time as restrictive covenants, violated the Constitution and could not be recognized by state courts.[30]

Organizations such as Strong Sr.'s rejoiced as the court's decisions upset rulings by the Supreme Courts of nineteen states, including Illinois. Several days later a Superior Court judge in Chicago denied a temporary injunction sought by the Park Manor Improvement Association to prevent an African American family from taking possession of a two-story brick residence on South Wabash Avenue. The gates of no housing opportunity had been shattered, but progress would be slow as the decades attested.

Before the 1950s could usher in a brighter spotlight on the game of basketball, Ted Jr. tied the knot in matrimony again. On April 23, 1949, thirty-two-year-old Ted Jr. married twenty-two-year-old Florence Faulkner in Chicago, with the Rev. J. H. Henderson officiating.[31]

"Yes, it was said that my uncle loved the nightlife and good-looking women," Terry Ellison, oldest grandson of Strong Sr., remarked. "I guess she was the one for him at that time."[32]

While Ted Jr. made a second attempt at marital bliss, new and younger African American players were emerging and beginning to move veterans like Ted Jr. to the edges of the Globetrotter spotlight. For years Ted Jr. held the distinction of having the largest hands in basketball. Kicking off the 1950 basketball season, the Ogden, Utah, *Standard-Examiner* featured a photograph of Nat "Sweetwater" Clifton, center for the Globetrotters, under the banner "Clifton Boasts Biggest Basketball Hands." A sports columnist for the newspaper noted that "the unit performing in Utah next week is the eastern unit, or the best of the two. The other unit is known as the western unit and features Ted Strong, Boyd Buie and others."[33]

Whether being relegated to the edges of the spotlight bothered Ted Jr. is uncertain. However, he took his basketball prowess and put it on display in North Dakota and Canada. In January 1950, Ted Jr. was in the lineup of the Minot All-American basketball club. He led the team with other former big-name team players such as Duane Markley, formerly of the House of David, in games against area teams. The January 28, 1950, edition of the *Bismarck Tribune* pictured Ted Jr. palming a basketball in the air under the headline "Stars for Minot." The caption read: "Ted Strong, former star of the famed Harlem Globetrotters, is one of the key members of the Minot All-Americans who will play the Bismarck Olympics here Tuesday. Strong teams with Fred Gran to give the All-Americans a strong scoring punch. In the first game between the two teams, the Olympics won, 57-52 at Minot."[34]

Ted Jr. became a fixture on a team that developed a heated rivalry with the area team the Bismarck Olympics. The games were so intense that the booking agent for the Minot All-Americans got off the bench during a game and punched a referee because he did not like a certain call. The booking agent spent time in jail on a disorderly conduct charge and was fined $25.

During Ted Jr.'s time with the All-Americans, his former boss and friend Abe Saperstein published a listing of the Globetrotters all-time "first squad." Ted Jr. was included, and the press used the information in articles. The North Dakota-Canada connection extended the playing careers of many former stars of nationally known teams, and Ted Jr. rode this connection in the winter months until the next baseball season opened.

Life seemed to have a peculiar way of working out with the Strongs when it came to sports. Ted Jr.'s reputation and remaining talent paved the way for him to join North Dakota's Minot Mallards of the newly formed ManDak Baseball League. A friend of Alvin Spearman's, Gentry Jessup, who played with the Birmingham Black Barons and the Chicago American Giants, told Spearman and the Strong brothers about a new league being formed in North Dakota that was paying more money than what they were receiving in the fading Negro Baseball Leagues.

> In 1950, the league consisted of the Winnipeg Buffaloes, the Winnipeg Elmwood Giants, the Carman Cardinals, the Bandon Greys and (in North Dakota) the Minot Mallards. Along with the Negro Leagues players, the ManDak League attracted a number of ex-major leaguers, minor league stars and some of the best Manitoba-, North Dakota- and Minnesota-born players. The talented young Negro players would go into organized baseball and the older players would journey north to Manitoba and North Dakota to continue their careers.[35]

During the baseball and basketball seasons, many of the players enjoyed the hospitality of area families who opened their doors to the sports figures they were reading about in the newspapers. They also stayed in local hotels and the YMCA. Ted Jr. was no exception. The hospitality and various arranged accommodations allowed him to transition from the basketball to the baseball season and remain in Canada as he joined the Minot Mallards as their first baseman. The ManDak League was in its infancy in 1950, and it did what it could to attract fans. What better way to attract fans than to secure the services of the greatest pitcher of the day—Leroy "Satchel" Paige—and what better way to help make it happen than to have Ted Jr., a buddy of Satchel's, egging him on to join the Minot Mallards? Well, Ted Jr. wasn't the only factor. A nice payday went a long way to bring the great Paige to Canada.

So, on Tuesday, May 30, 1950, Satchel Paige pitched three innings and helped the Mallards defeat the Brandon Greys 4–3 before a large Memorial Day crowd. The great Satchel struck out seven of the nine batters he faced while his former Monarch teammate Ted Jr. scored the third Minot run by singling to right field "advancing to second on Ev Faunce's safe bunt, and reaching home as a wild throw by Grey's catcher, Lenny Pigg. Faunce scored the winning run on Del Triplett's single."[36]

The Minot Mallards were competing well for the league title against the Winnipeg Buffaloes and Brandon Greys. Ted Jr. contributed in virtually every game he played. In early June, he helped his club to a third-straight victory by defeating the Carman Cardinals 7–4.[37]

In early July, the ManDak League launched tournament play, and even though the Mallards didn't take home the title, Ted Jr. homered for Minot. It would be Ted Jr.'s last hit for the Mallards. The *Winnipeg Free Press* reported in its Monday, July 30, 1950, edition that "the Mallards lost Ted Strong and Len Williams when the pair jumped to the Switt Current Sask club."[38] Why Ted Jr. left the Mallards is unknown.

Ted Jr. resurfaced with the man he knew most of his life: Abe Saperstein. Basketball season was about to start, but there was something else on the horizon of which Abe felt that Ted Jr. should be a part. For months Columbia Pictures had writers working on a script for a movie about the internationally famous Globetrotters. Saperstein wanted to gain more attention for his enterprise, and he had been negotiating with contacts in the movie industry to have a movie produced. The wheels were turning, and Saperstein learned that production would start just before the team left the United States for an overseas tour. When talking about the Harlem Globetrotters and its history, Saperstein knew that he needed to have Ted Jr. in the movie playing himself. From the days of Wendell Phillips High School to sitting in Strong Sr.'s living room attempting to convince the elder Strong to let Ted Jr. join Saperstein's basketball squad to the countless victories the Globetrotters amassed, there was Ted Jr. How could Saperstein not have Ted Jr. with other pillars of the Globetrotters appearing in such a movie? It was only right.

Columbia Pictures began shooting *The Harlem Globetrotters* on Friday, October 13, 1950, in Hollywood. The news release that the Globetrotters circulated to newspapers around the country said that the story "will be built around the experiences of a new rookie on the squad, and the Saperstein method of forming the greatest basketball aggregation in the world—a team that has been playing now for 23 years, with a record of 3,241 games won and only 245 lost."[39]

For two weeks, Ted Jr. joined a group of Globetrotters acting in the production of the seventy-eight-minute, black-and-white movie that starred Hollywood's first African American movie star, Dorothy Dandridge, in her second major role. Ted Jr. played himself in the movie, acting out scenes on the basketball floor and in locker rooms that illustrated the life of basketball players finding ways to win in the sport they loved.

On October 24, 1951, Columbia Pictures released the film nationwide. The movie studio was so impressed with the final cut of the movie, directed by first-time director Phil Brown and producer Buddy Adler, that "it gave the film a double A rating, meaning it would be promoted as if it were a million-dollar film, although it had cost only $250,000."[40] When the movie opened, it received favorable reviews and high praise from people in the African American community, who flocked to the theaters to witness the story of their team. And, for members of the Strong family, the pride of seeing their famous brother on the big screen was just a mind-blower.

"Oh, man, seeing my big brother on that big screen just made me so proud," Jasper Strong recalled. "No one else I knew in my neighborhood could say they had their brother in the movies."[41]

"I didn't see it when it first came out, but I saw it years later and it was good," said Larry Lester, noted Negro Leagues baseball historian.[42]

Before syndication became a household word, the film made the drive-in theater circuits, which helped to extend its life well into 1952 and beyond. Abe Saperstein Enterprises received a percentage of the film's gross. While the Globetrotters gained modest attention internationally, the U.S. government boosted the image of the team by using it as propaganda to paint a different picture of U.S. race relations. Specific scenes in the movie were described in reviews by the U.S. Information Service as showing African Americans being welcomed in public places and enjoying a carefree cosmopolitan lifestyle.[43]

Unfortunately, the U.S. propaganda efforts couldn't outdo the real-life saga that was occurring in the 1950s. Due to the rise of McCarthyism that was fueled and engulfed by the Communist hysteria, the director and producer of *The Harlem Globetrotters* were blacklisted, and Ted Jr. and the other players were "forced to stay in a 'colored' hotel in Los Angeles."[44] Yes, Ted Jr. was a "movie star" now, but what he received in compensation remains a mystery. The contract that Abe Saperstein had with Columbia Pictures required him, rather than the studio, to pay Ted Jr. and the other players, "supposedly at the minimum rates in the Screen Actors Guild contract."[45] If Ted Jr. had asked for an advance of his salary to accommodate for expenses while in Los Angeles, he might have owed Saperstein after the movie production ended.

In April 1952, the Globetrotters undertook their most ambitious feat when they embarked on their annual international tour. Instead of playing eighteen games in seventeen cities as they had done in 1950, they were scheduled to do 141 games in 168 days.

"This is going to be the greatest tour in sports history," Abe declared, and who could possibly disagree? On April 19, 1952, one unit of Trotters flew to Panama and played the next five weeks in Latin America. On May 30, the main entourage—twenty-nine people, including eleven Trotters, the New York Celtics (led by Red Klotz and Tony

Lavelli, who also played accordion at halftime), two referees, four half-time acts, plus Abe, Gottlieb, Kennedy, and Zinkoff—left New York for the European leg of the tour. Goose Tatum and Sweetwater Clifton planned to join up with the team later, due to family illness. Abe had bought two buses and had them shipped over ahead of time, along with his red Cadillac. "To add a touch of class," he would say, which would draw crowds wherever they went.[46]

This worldwide tour took the Globetrotters to another level unparalleled in sports history. It would have been another source of pride for members of the Strong family had Ted Jr. made the trip. However, several days after his thirty-fifth birthday, Ted Jr. received his appointment to begin working as a clerk at the U.S. Post Office in Chicago. He entered at Grade 2 for $1.66 per hour. Ted Jr. probably learned of the job from other African Americans who put in a good word for him since a number of former Negro Leagues players had landed postal jobs. Ted Jr. needed the paycheck, but a man of his stature would find it hard not to be in the spotlight when he would read about how overseas the Globetrotters were kings and basking in the admiration and wide-eyed enchantment they brought to the thousands of international fans who just couldn't get enough of the basketball wizards.

One afternoon in the fall of 1952, Othello and Ted Jr. stopped by to see their father, who had moved into an apartment after separating from Vera. While sitting in the parlor of their father's apartment enjoying a soda and chatting, they learned that their father was dating a young woman named Ernestine Briscoe. She was friends with their sister Gwendolyn. The twenty-nine-year-old Ernestine had been impressed with the tall, stately gentleman who was well known in the community. At the age of fifty-eight, he was good-looking too.

The sons just shrugged and listened as the father inquired about how things were going in their lives. Ted Jr. talked about the Globetrotter tour, and Othello mentioned the season he had in Canada and the ManDak League. The talk about the ManDak League prompted Strong Sr. to discuss the Negro Leagues and their declining stature in the community. Although he had retired from participating in Negro Leagues baseball activities in 1948, Strong Sr. still had opinions about the Negro Baseball Leagues, and he wanted to inform his sons about some things that he knew were unknown to them. One particular aspect was the integration of the white and black baseball leagues.

"It wasn't from Branch Rickey's goodness. It was because we had organized and set up a plan to set up a league," Strong Sr. said. "Johnson in Mounds, Illinois, was going to help me to break the color-line in the National and American Leagues."[47]

Strong Sr. felt the Negro Leagues helped to cause their own demise by not working independently of "outside" groups: "I debated with Dr. Martin and others in 1937 that I wanted Bingo DeMoss to do certain things, and they wanted Saperstein as our booking agent. They debated me down, and Saperstein within two to three years owned part of Cleveland and other teams. I stood there that February morning and argued down that I didn't want Saperstein. At that time I was part owner of Indianapolis ABCs in the Negro American League, and that's why I walked out of baseball because they thought they couldn't get by without whites being predominant figures."[48]

Ted Jr. and Othello listened and occasionally nodded their heads in agreement. They knew their father had history that many people in their circle of friends could only dream about. They had heard these stories before, but they never tired of listening. His knowledge helped them excel since he had been where they were going. The sons knew they were fortunate and blessed. Their father was the head of the house, and he, like many African American fathers of the 1950s, tried to explain the ins and outs of life, as well as be a role model. This was the era before the demise of the black family structure that began in the 1960s with the advent of welfare. Fathers were part of the fabric of African American life unless they were killed or run from the home by white racists attempting to keep African Americans in their place.

Strong Sr. would also find time to slip in some discussion regarding current events; he was so passionate about the plight of African Americans. He railed about the vices that kept African Americans in bondage, as he would say, and the activities of the South Side policy kings consistently attracted his attention. The *Chicago Defender* would report on the activities of the mob and policy kings:

> Two "front men" for the mob which took over the Boulevard-Avenue policy wheels with machine guns, three weeks ago, were fined $200 each Saturday, after being re-arrested Friday in a raid on the wheel headquarters, 3034 Indiana Avenue.[49]

Months later, an editorial by the *Defender* spoke about the death of the "last of Chicago's great policy kings":

> Theodore "Ted" Row, the last of Chicago's great policy kings is dead, the victim of assassins' bullets. His death, brings to a close an era that

was born during the rise of the notorious Al Capone to unprecedented gangland power.

Chicago was the only city where the lush policy racket was controlled by Negroes. Though most of those who rose to places of power either met with violent deaths or were run out of the racket by threats of violence, as a group, in spite of rivalries and personal differences they never resorted to violence.

Theirs was a lush era with a seeming unending flow of cash pouring into the luxuries and frivolities of life. It had one redeeming feature. Some of the profits did find their way into legitimate channels—small businesses and real estate especially, and some was spent for charitable purposes.

None of these men, however, was of a type one would like to have his children emulate.

Their flagrant disregard for the law, their corruption of officials, their catering to the gambling instincts of many who could not afford to gamble, their brazen defiance of decency were acts that stamped them as men working against the common good.

Whether or not the death of Roe marks the end of the era of policy or marks just a change in control of the racket, as many believe, policy should and must go.[50]

Strong Sr. knew it would be an uphill battle against the problems plaguing the African American community, but he also expressed hope and exhorted his children to fight for what they believed was right.

The African American community continued its efforts for jobs, equality, and justice, spurred on by crusades in the *Chicago Defender*. The crusades initiated by the *Defender* offered hope and encouraged African Americans in Chicago to press harder for more gains.

That was "okay news" to Strong Sr., but it wasn't enough. His sons knew he could get on a roll, so they would gradually shift the conversation back to sports. Baseball was the love of each man, and the activities of African American men in the World Series became center stage. Jackie Robinson hit his first homer for the Brooklyn Dodgers in a World Series against the New York Yankees. And the twenty-eight-year-old, right-handed relief pitcher Joe Black made his third appearance as a starting pitcher for the Dodgers.

In boxing, another sport that Strong Sr. loved, he and other African Americans were disappointed that Rocky Marciano defeated Jersey Joe Walcott in a grueling battle that ended in the thirteenth round when Marciano exploded a superb right hook against the jaw of the heavyweight champion. With Walcott's defeat, an era in boxing came to an end. Not since June 22, 1937, had a white fighter held the heavyweight champion-ship belt. African Americans were hoping Walcott could become the first fighter to regain the title.

As 1952 came to an end, Strong Sr. and Vera remained separated, liv-ing apart but still caring for their children. Twenty-one-year-old Thaddeus was serving in the military; Ted Jr. was about to turn thirty-six years old in January; and Othello was in his prime at twenty-six. However, the year ended on a sad note. Former Newark Eagles baseball club owner Abraham (Abe) Manley died at the age of sixty-seven following a prolonged illness. Mr. Manley's Eagles were instrumental in the baseball careers of several major league stars—Larry Doby, Monte Irvin, and Don Newcombe, all of whom were former stars of the Eagles. Manley was credited with helping to organize the Negro National League, never having his team finish a season out of the first division, and capturing the 1946 Negro Leagues World Se-ries. The last credit remained etched in Ted Jr.'s memory . . . unfortunately.

The first five months of 1953 didn't bode well for Ted Jr. Accord-ing to Cook County, Illinois, Divorce Division court proceedings held in 1967, Ted Jr.'s wife, Florence, testified that on Tuesday, March 17, 1953, he left and never returned to their home. The marriage difficulties prob-ably contributed to Ted Jr. only sporadically showing up for work at the Chicago post office. When he should have been at work, he would handle small assignments for Abe Saperstein and Inman Jackson at the Globetrot-ters' headquarters. He also spent a great deal of time enjoying the night life. The world of sports and the glamour and prestige that came with it was hard for him to leave. Being a former sports figure didn't matter to his supervisors. He was hired to perform his duties at the post office, but his absences increased, and finally the assistant postmaster general wrote a let-ter on May 15, 1953, ordering the removal of Ted Jr. due to absence from duty without leave.

It is uncertain what the remainder of the 1950s held for Ted Jr. He would pick up odd jobs here and there and occasionally receive some help from Abe Saperstein and other friends and relatives who just liked the guy. While Ted Jr.'s star had descended, his younger brother Othello became a source of pride for the Strong family.

11

TED JR.'S YOUNGER BROTHER BEGINS TO "BREAK 'EM" OFF

Othello Strong, born March 12, 1926, in Chicago as the seventh child of Strong Sr. and his wife, Vera, followed in the footsteps of his now-famous brother. Several years after the birth of Othello, the Strong family moved to 4819 Langley, where young Othello and his older brothers and sisters adapted to their new surroundings. It wasn't long before Othello met a short and outgoing young man like himself named Morris Gordon, and a lifelong friendship evolved. The Gordon family lived nearby at 4823 Langley, and the proximity encouraged the two boys' friendship. "We would sit out on the porch of our apartment building and talk. We would also play baseball day and night in Washington Park," remembered Morris.[1]

Washington Park was one of the havens for African Americans in the Black Belt to gather for picnics, to enjoy the many lagoons, and to participate or watch other African Americans play baseball. "We started playing in the streets of our neighborhood until we decided to go to Washington Park at 51st Street and play older boys," Gordon said with a smile. "My older brother Charles, Alvin Spearman, Robert and Herbert Wooley, myself, and Othello decided to form a team. We felt that we were pretty good."[2]

Twelve-year-old Othello gave them the confidence to create a team. Strong Sr. showed Othello how to throw a curve ball in keeping with his practice of teaching his boys the games he loved—baseball and basketball. Gordon and his brothers knew that Othello's father had been a baseball player, and they got a kick out of discovering that Strong Sr. had played for the Zulu Giants, a semiprofessional baseball team, leading to Othello's nickname from his friends. "We started calling Othello 'Zulu' because of the team his father played with," Gordon laughed. "We thought it was funny and between us guys the nickname stuck."[3] Armed with Othello's developing curve ball and a zealous desire to win, the boys journeyed to different vacant lots on the South Side and any open city park and took on all challengers.

"By Othello knowing how to throw a curve ball, that moved us up to play the bigger boys," Gordon said. "Look like we beat everybody because Othello knew how to throw a curve. The ball would be breakin' and the boys couldn't do anything with it."[4] Gordon served as the catcher. He had years of training from catching for his older brothers who all wanted to be pitchers. As the youngest, Gordon was routinely relegated to catcher. "I didn't mind catching Othello, though. Man, could he throw that curve."[5] Gordon recalled one particular game with some pride when his lanky, right-handed pitcher friend showed his stuff. "We went to 33rd and Rhodes where there was a ball field, and Othello really threw a no-hitter as a teenager. I did the catching but he got all the credit, which he deserved. We just made a name for ourselves."[6]

After success in defeating neighborhood teams, the boys went back to Washington Park to observe the Industrial Leagues, composed of teams sponsored by the many meatpacking companies from the famous Chicago Stock Yards. The Industrial Leagues were a fixture of the Washington Park landscape. African American kids like Othello and his friend Gordon honed their baseball skills watching the Industrial League teams play. "The guys were older than we were. They would let us younger kids serve as bat boys and fetch foul balls and all that. As we got older they let us play with them. And were they surprised when Othello started to pitch and breaking that curve. They couldn't do a darn thing with it."[7] Othello used the skills he learned from his father and Ted Jr. and the training he received in the vacant lots and parks of the Black Belt to gain notoriety for himself. Finally, one of the Industrial League teams called on Othello.

"Lakeview Dairy Company had a team, and they asked us to play with them. They asked Othello to pitch, and, believe me, he drew the crowds as he threw that curve," Gordon said with pride.[8]

The Strong and Gordon family members went to Washington Park and joined other African Americans to watch Othello demonstrate his pitching prowess and Gordon show off his catching abilities. "I modeled myself after Frank Duncan who was a catcher with the Negro Leagues," Gordon said. "I would say 'I'm Duncan' and I would mimic the catching of my hero."

One day the manager of the Lakeview Dairy team asked Othello, Gordon, and their other friends to join the team as it traveled to Joliet, Illinois, and Joliet State Prison to play the prison team. Always willing to accept a challenge, the boys took the hour bus ride to Joliet, southwest of Chicago. As the game progressed, the warden of the prison wanted to inspire his team.

"The Warden told the prison team that whoever got a home run would get two weeks off from work. Believe me, he shouldn't have said that because they kept hitting that ball over the fence. It seemed like every time Othello would throw, they would knock it out of the park. Man, we got a laugh out of that. But the next year, we went back, and we had gotten stronger and older and it was a different ball game."[9]

Despite the barrage of home runs, the boys pitched, hit, and fielded their way to a victory over the Joliet prison team. They were excelling in the game they loved. As the years progressed, the boys gravitated to more sports interests. Othello's buddy Morris joined the DuSable basketball team in his sophomore year while Othello continued to hone his skills playing with Industrial League baseball teams and squads put together by owners of small businesses in the Black Belt. Othello's other buddy Alvin Spearman (who would go on to have a successful pitching career in the Negro Leagues and with minor league squads in the white leagues), joined DuSable's football team and excelled as a halfback from 1943 to 1945.[10]

Early on, Al and Othello—or "Odie" as Al affectionately called his pal—recognized that they were both a stride ahead of the pack when they met. "He and I seemed to be outstanding, and we immediately bonded," Spearman remarked. "We played all kinds of sports in the vacant lots and in Washington Park."[11] Al lived at 4827 Langley, and he attended Willard Elementary School with Othello and his other buddies. He grew up with the Strong clan, and he experienced life in the Black Belt that burned lasting memories. As teenagers and active athletes on the school's various sports teams, Othello, Spearman, and their buddies were popular with the opposite sex. For Spearman, the attraction led to the birth of two sons by his girlfriend. Typical of any teenage environment, small talk among the girls and boys often led to potential problems. "Ollie and Charlotte Strong and the mother of my two sons ran together," Spearman said. "At school there was a girl who took a liking to me, and we began to share a locker. Well, Charlotte told my sons' mother about it, and I got mad. I confronted Charlotte and told her that she should mind her own damn business. Next thing I knew, Nathaniel Strong, who was four years older than I and who graduated from DuSable with my brother in 1942, got mad at me and wanted to fight."[12]

Spearman enjoyed a number of sports. About the time he and Othello met at the age of thirteen, he convinced the Chicago Golden Gloves representatives to accept him in the tournament as a sixteen-year-old. He boxed for several years and achieved some success. Even with that boxing experience, Spearman had no desire to fight Nathaniel "in the streets," as he put it. The matter blew over, and the friends moved on.

World events smoothed over the matter sooner as the Selective Service draft net swung around again and nabbed Othello in February 1945. He was nineteen years old. A month later, Spearman's number was called, and he entered the army on the heels of his buddy Odie.

Othello's time in the military is sketchy. His military records and millions of others were destroyed on July 12, 1973, after a disastrous fire at the National Personnel Records Center (NPRC). What has been learned about his time in the service is that the young right-hander used his magnificent curve ball to baffle opponents at Fort Warren in Wyoming. He obviously honed his skills since news reports repeatedly published his exploits on the pitching mound. Fort Warren featured many outstanding baseball teams, and Othello fit right in. In October 1946 when he received his separation papers from the army, Othello's big brother Ted Jr. made a call to Abe Saperstein, who was recruiting players for a Harlem Globetrotter baseball squad. Othello became an instant hit and one of the leading pitchers of the club.

Saperstein used his connections with the African American baseball community to create the team. One of the managers was Paul Hardy, who formerly played for the Birmingham Black Barons. Other Negro Leaguers on the team were shortstop Jesse Williams of the Kansas City Monarchs and second baseman Henry Smith, formerly of the Indianapolis Clowns.

The excitement of Othello's entry into professional sports was heightened after the emergence of Jackie Robinson. If Ted Jr.'s prospects were slim for the white leagues, maybe Othello could pick up the torch. Having just turned twenty-one, and possessing a right arm that could unleash a wicked curve, the possibilities for Othello Strong looked bright—if given the right seasoning with Saperstein's team and the Negro Baseball Leagues.

As these advancements and opportunities brought hope to the African American community, the Strong family could also smile as Othello Strong continued his rise in sports. The young, lanky right-hander, now standing six-feet-two-inches, was taking his superb curve ball and making a number of would-be hitters, as famed Chicago White Sox baseball announcer Ken "Hawk" Harrelson would say, "grab some bench" after failing to lay any wood on the disappearing ball.

Playing baseball for the Harlem Globetrotters allowed Othello the opportunity to see the country like his big brother Ted Jr., or "Jeep" as he was known by his Indianapolis Clowns teammates. In June 1948, Othello traveled with the Globetrotters to Denver, en route to the Pacific Coast to open a series with the Honolulu Hawaiians. While in Colorado, the team scored 9–6 and 11–7 wins against the Coors of Golden, Colorado, the national semipro champions and winners of the Denver Post National Baseball Tournament in 1947.

In August 1948, Othello and teammates were in West Virginia, where they competed in an exhibition game against the Hawaiians. In one game Othello won a 3–1 decision over the burly Ernie Cabral, who was known for his blazing fastball. The *Charleston Gazette* enthused that Othello "is touted as one of the coming greats among Negro pitchers. His two-year record with the Trotters as a hurler since leaving Fort Warren has been most impressive."[13]

During the remainder of the 1948 baseball season, Othello racked up wins for the Trotters while his brother Ted Jr. played games here and there with the Globetrotters to make money after his suspension from the Clowns. Ted Jr.'s connection with Abe Saperstein allowed him to play baseball with the Globetrotters unit. Othello's impressive showings opened the door for greater opportunities, and in February 1949 the Chicago American Giants announced that they had signed him to a contract. Othello joined the team and headed south to Monroe, Louisiana, for exhibition games against the Houston Eagles on March 26. The Chicago American Giants defeated the Eagles in both games, and Othello could only revel in his chance in the Negro Leagues as his childhood buddy, Alvin Spearman, joined him on the team.

The 1949 season opener on Sunday, May 1, at Comiskey Park saw the Giants play the Baltimore Elite Giants. As always, Strong Sr. took his family to the ballpark to cheer on Odie. Strong Sr. beamed at the opportunity to watch his son prepare for the season opener while he chatted with family friends like Ted "Double Duty" Radcliffe. "Yes, we saw all those guys," Jasper Strong reminisced. "Double Duty used to own a liquor store down the street from where we were living, and my brothers would take me and I would sit and have a soda while they talked."[14]

The Chicago American Giants started the season blazing. They won six out of seven games. The Giants continued their winning ways as they traveled into Kansas City to face the mighty Monarchs in a doubleheader. Big innings in both games sealed the victories for the Giants as they strolled to 8–2 and 9–5. Such victories paved the way for the Giants to take the second half of the 1949 season.

Unfortunately, Othello did not play with the Giants after the second half of the season ended. He returned to the Harlem Globetrotters baseball squad, touring and playing such teams as the Cinderella Sports, an African American semiprofessional team in Monroe, Louisiana; the Cincinnati Crescents, another African American semiprofessional team; and the Hawaii Stars of Honolulu. He played in cities such as Ogden, Utah; Council Bluffs, Iowa; Charleston, West Virginia; Denver; and Altoona, Pennsylvania. Why Othello did not complete the second half of the 1949 season with the Giants is unknown. The Giants certainly could have used his superb curve ball. The Giants reached the playoffs against the Baltimore Elites; however, the Elites swept the Giants in four games.

The change in sports mimicked the change in seasons as baseball gave way to basketball. This particular year would be beneficial to one of the Strong brothers when a shakeup in ownership of the Chicago American Giants occurred in December 1949. Ownership of various Negro Leagues baseball teams changed hands. J. B. Martin, president of the Negro American League, relinquished his control of the Chicago American Giants to Chicago businessman William Little. As part of this deal R. S. Simmons, a protégé of the legendary Andrew (Rube) Foster, was named general manager, and Ted "Double Duty" Radcliffe was named manager. Double Duty succeeded Winfield Welch, who managed the Giants in 1949.

Returning to Chicago, Othello reengaged with the Giants for the 1950 baseball season and posted a decent record. Unfortunately, the 1950 season for the Giants was a complete reversal of the 1949 campaign.

The campaign started well for Othello. In Memphis, during a doubleheader in Martin Stadium in May 1950, Othello scattered eight hits while his teammates tallied a lead that allowed him to win easily 9–3. The nightcap saw the Memphis Red Sox nip the Giants 4–3. Several weeks later, the Giants returned to Comiskey Park to face the 1949 Negro Leagues champion Baltimore Elite Giants in a Sunday doubleheader. Only 3,500 people witnessed the affair as Baltimore edged the Giants in the first game 6–5. In the second game, Othello used his superb curve and off-speed pitches to hold the Elite Giants to four hits to record his fourth victory of the year as the American Giants won 1–0.

As Othello racked wins, the African American press took note, and Othello's name began to appear on the note pads of fans and sportswriters anticipating the annual East-West All-Star Game in August. Othello's name appeared as a likely candidate for pitching honors along with others, such as Elston Howard, Kansas City Monarch outfielder; Birmingham Black Barons center fielder Willie Mays; and Art Pennington, the center fielder for the Chicago American Giants.

The Negro Leagues slowly descended from their glory days, and teams took on other teams wherever they could find them. The Chicago American Giants played the Kokomo Boosters in a night game in Kokomo, Indiana, where the local newspaper pumped up the event by mentioning, "21-year-old Othello Strong has given the hill crops a tremendous boost." The newspaper, in a later edition, printed a picture of young Othello completing his pitching motion above the caption:

> He May Be The Boy—Hard-throwing Othello Strong, the newest edition to the ranks of the pitching "regular" with the Chicago American Giants was a good bet for Manager Ted Radcliffe's starting nod against the Kokomo Boosters at Highland Park Thursday night. The 21-year-old Strong, a product of the Chicago sandlots, has been one of the brightest rookies in the Negro American league this year. Thursday's game was slated for 8:30 o'clock.[15]

The young, tall, dark-skinned ballplayer felt he was on top of the world. The notoriety expanded his confidence, and the attention attracted the opposite sex in ways that could make other men envious. Now as a grown man, Othello could set sail on his own and experience what life had to offer. As a professional athlete, he was destined to see things no mere young African American would ever dream of experiencing.

The Black Belt contained everything a young man could want—fine restaurants, hotels, parks, churches, retail stores, and nightclubs galore. Those distractions had to be mentally minimized in order to focus on the task of playing baseball for Giant manager Double Duty, who wanted discipline. He wanted you to play your heart out because even at the ripe age of forty-nine, he could get on the field and embarrass a player.

This 1950s team began to show that it didn't have what the 1949 team had. The Giants returned to Chicago for two doubleheaders against former teams of Ted Jr. The Giants and Othello didn't fare well against either team. On July 9, the Indianapolis Clowns defeated them 7–1 and 11–0. A week later the Kansas City Monarchs came to Comiskey Park and strolled away victorious. In the first game, Othello relived teammate Harry Rhodes, whom the Monarchs tagged for six runs in two innings. Othello couldn't stop the onslaught. He yielded ten hits over the remaining innings in a 13–1 loss. The second game ended in a 3–0 win for the Monarchs in front of approximately five thousand fans. The slide continued weeks later in Baltimore against the Elite Giants, who were the second-half leaders in the Eastern Division of the Negro American League. The Elites clobbered

Othello and company 13–5 and 9–5. In the opener, the Elites battered Othello and his pitching mate Harold Gordon for twelve runs. Circumstances didn't improve for the Chicago American Giants. They finished the 1950 campaign in last place in the Negro American League West Division with a 15–31 record.

As the elder Strong's life evolved, so did the life of his youngest baseball-playing son. Othello, along with thirty-four other players, was ordered to report to the Chicago American Giants spring training camp in Meridian, Mississippi, in April 1951. The Giants manager Winfield Welch told the *Baltimore Afro-American* that he was counting on eight pitching prospects to make the Giants a contender for the Negro American League pennant. The list included Othello and his childhood buddy Alvin Spearman. Othello and Spearman showed good promise during the spring exhibition contests for the Giants. They entered the 1951 season opener for the Giants at home at Comiskey Park in May, and the newspaper buzzed about the game, focusing on Satchel Paige. Paige had left the major leagues after declining to accept the contract offered by the Cleveland Indians due to a cut in his salary.

The Chicago Giants faithful were ready to see a marvelous performance by Paige when the Giants faced their second Sunday home doubleheader against the Indianapolis Clowns. Ted Jr. had recently joined the Clowns for another baseball stint, and this would be the first encounter that featured both Strongs in the lineup for opposing teams. (Othello's buddy Alvin Spearman left the Giants and moved to Canada to join the Carman Cardinals where he had a 5–5 pitching record.) Both teams got off to a tremendous start with the Giants sporting a 13–3 record and Indianapolis amassing a 12–2 mark. The Giants would battle well into the 1951 campaign. The team finished with a 21–16 record in the first half and managed to scratch a 13–8 record in the second half, finishing behind the eventual pennant winning Kansas City Monarchs. Othello participated through three-quarters of the season before jumping to the ManDak League in Canada and the Winnipeg Buffaloes. Whether it was a change of scenery, more money, or lesser talent, Othello excelled, as news reports showed:

The *Brandon Daily Sun*, Thursday, August 2, 1951, Page 2
"Carman, Minot Score Mandak Wins"
Othello Strong, a new recruit from Chicago, and formerly with Minot, homered for Winnipeg in the third with none on. Minot defeated Winnipeg 7 to 4.

Winnipeg Free Press, **August 7, 1951, Page 20**
"Buffs Bounce Carman, 15-8"
Willie's "pitcher in left field," Othello Strong, was a hitting demon
against the Cards, smashing four singles and a double in five official bats.
He also walked.

Winnipeg Free Press, **August 13, 1951, Page 16**
"Carman Wins Tough On Giants"
Delivering in the first were Othello Strong, Cal Miles and Buddy Owens. Strong and Miles added a second homer each during the fray and
for good measure Strong tossed in a triple and single good for six runs
batted in.

Meanwhile at Minot, Carman's Cards, bent on holding onto the
fourth spot, whipped Minot 10-3 Saturday, and then coasted to a 4-1
win Sunday behind Al Spearman's fine one-hit hurling chore.

Winnipeg Free Press, **August 18, 1951, Page 21**
Buffs Win In Final Frame
Winnipeg Buffaloes scored four runs in the top of the ninth to down
Carman Friday night. The Herd broke the deadlock in the final frame
as they got to Gene Smith for four hits, four runs, and the ball game.

Until that time, the towering pitcher was the hero of the game. Besides turning in a workman-like hurling job for the first eight innings,
Smith clouted a three-run homer in the second to give the Redbirds
their only runs.

But the right-handed fireball weakened badly in the final frame to allow Othello Strong to nose out the fourth-place Cards in another close
one. Just 10 evenings before, the stringbean hurler downed the Cards
in 10 innings.

Winnipeg Free Press, **September 3, 1951, Page 15**
"Willie Watches While Buffs Win"
Coming up with the catches of the night were Othello Strong, who
hobbled under a fast failing blooper off the bat of Jako and then retired
to the sidelines.

Winnipeg Free Press, **September 6, 1951, Page 21**
"Mallard Bats Bounce Buffs 6-2"
Othello Strong, who pitches sometimes but played left field Wednesday,
hit three-for-four with two singles and a homer.

Othello and the Buffaloes drove hard to capture first place in the
ManDak League's standings. However, the Brandon Greys edged them

out, leading to the best of seven playoff series. The Winnipeg team squared off against the third-place Minot Mallards while the Greys played the Carman Cardinals.

Even though Othello had gained the reputation as an excellent pitcher, he had rounded into a good hitter as well, and his skill with the bat helped the Buffaloes take one of the playoff games from the Mallards. The Buffaloes won the playoff series from the Mallards and met the Brandon Greys in the finals. The Brandon team demonstrated why they snagged the league title. They swept Othello and the Buffaloes 4–0.

Othello had a good run with the Buffaloes for the 1951 campaign. He proved that the reports about him were not exaggerated. He just needed to play in a league that would pay him more than what the diminishing Negro Leagues could pay. After the season ended, Othello returned to Chicago and picked up odd jobs, while his brother did his usual routine and reconnected with the Globetrotters. Ted Jr. was still a fan favorite, and after the successful run of the Harlem Globetrotter movie, more basketball fans turned out to see the heroes of the big screen.

While Ted Jr. continued to be the talk of the family and the neighborhood in Bronzeville, Othello headed back to the ManDak League in May for the 1952 season. Upon returning to Winnipeg, he learned that the team was now called the Giants instead of the Buffaloes. It didn't matter to Othello as long as he received a decent paycheck. He just went about his business playing baseball the way his father had taught him. In June the Giants played the Minot Mallards, and although they were narrowly beaten 17–15, Othello batted in six runs and smashed two home runs.

He continued where he had left off in 1951 by, at times, single-handedly dragging his team back from the brink of defeat.

Brandon Daily Sun, June 9, 1952, Page 2
"Othello Strong Hurls, Bats Giants To Win Over Cards
Lanky Hurler Drives Home Winning
Run To Climax Comeback"
WINNIPEG, JUNE 9 (CP)—The pitching and hitting of Othello Strong Saturday night gave the Winnipeg Giants a 4–3 victory over the Carman Cardinals in a Mandak baseball league game here.

Strong's scratch single to left field in the ninth inning sent Nick Cannull scampering for home with the winning run. It capped a Giant comeback that saw the Winnipeg team come from behind a 3–1 count to tie it in the eighth and win in the ninth.

Fred Brenzel went all the way for Carman, scattering six hits, three by Strong. Other Giant hitters were Wmmet Willson, Louie Louden and Cannuli.

Youthful Arnie Boushy was the only Cardinal to manage more than one hit off Strong. The Winnipeg hurler gave up seven hits, struck out seven and walked one.

However, Othello's 1952 season in the ManDak League was short-lived. Less than a month later, the *Winnipeg Free Press* indicated that the Giants announced, "Ted Radcliffe, who was released by the Giants Saturday, and Othello Strong, pitcher and left fielder, have been suspended indefinitely by the league. Strong jumped the Giants to go with Radcliffe when he left."[16]

Othello was on track to have an outstanding season. The following week the ManDak League released its statistics for the mid-year. A hard-hitting outfielder for the Carman Cardinals held the top spot in the league batting race with Othello just behind his pitching buddy Gentry Jessup of the Cardinals with batting numbers of .404 and .364 respectively. Unfortunately, Othello and Gentry hadn't been at the plate often enough to qualify for the honors.

There must have been opportunities elsewhere, and Radcliffe, who had connections, was just the man Othello needed. Othello supposedly surfaced in Albuquerque, though the report of his arrival left many people scratching their heads:

Albuquerque Journal, **August 5, 1952, Page 16**
"Borger Falls To De Carolis; Priest Faces Sox"
Othello Strong, Negro pitcher signed last week, is on the missing persons list. [Cy] Fausett [team owner] can't contact him in Chicago and has no idea as to whether or not he is en-route here.

In August 1952 Othello Strong was twenty-six years old, single, good-looking, and a talented athlete, able to capitalize on promising opportunities whenever and wherever they arose. Interspersed between his travels to different cities for baseball, Othello made efforts to return to Chicago because he had a special interest that had recently developed in his life. At an event in Chicago during the winter of 1952, he met a lovely, olive-skinned African American woman who grabbed his heart immediately. Jacqueline Harris was twenty years old and single. She thought this tall, lanky man was just looking for his next conquest, and she did her best to give him the impression that she wasn't interested. Fate had other plans, and the two began courting. Jackie, as she became known, believed she had found the man of her life, and Othello liked her because she was different from other women he had met up to that point in his life.

While Othello loved having a special woman in his life, he also enjoyed baseball and the freedom it brought him as he traveled to city after city competing against area baseball teams. And he relished the attention that an athlete received, especially from the opposite sex. Employment opportunities for African Americans were opening up somewhat, but any African American male who had athletic skills was still in a better financial position than the African American male working in a factory or piecing together odd jobs. The athlete was revered in the community, and if he had the looks to go along with it, chances are his selections of the opposite sex were abundant and difficult to resist.

12

TWILIGHT TRIPLE HEADER

Ted Jr. and other family members had no way of knowing that the remainder of the 1950s would be the launching pad for more African American struggles for freedom, justice, and equality in America. Ted Jr. and Othello began 1953 by evaluating their chances with various baseball traveling teams. Othello knew he stood a better chance than his brother. Youth was in his favor; he was a good ten years younger than his older sibling. He talked with good friends like Double Duty and Al Spearman and decided to try out for the West Texas–New Mexico League. In March 1953, Othello signed with the Albuquerque Dukes, where he had a mediocre season.

Life on the road for an African American athlete was notoriously difficult. Unreliable transportation, Jim Crow laws in the South that made hotel accommodations near to impossible, and the inadequate salaries complicated life to the point of questioning the reason for staying with the sport. And to top it all, Othello had the love of his life who wanted more of his life than she was receiving. After weighing his options, Othello determined that he would hang up his cleats at the end of the 1953 season. In Chicago on January 15, 1954, Othello L. Strong married Jacqueline Harris. Othello retired to the South Side of Chicago with Jacqueline and found a job working as a truck driver for Careful Cleaners.

Ted Jr. slowly faded into the memory of the sports world as the years progressed. He occasionally would be part of various recognition ceremonies arranged by Abe Saperstein and Inman Jackson. He would attend Globetrotter sporting events with former teammates. At the Chicago Stadium, they would watch the newer version of the Globetrotters compete against a less lustrous Minneapolis Lakers, who now had big George Mikan as coach.

He worked as a consultant for Saperstein on small projects but never to the extent of Inman Jackson, who worked with Abe and the organization until Saperstein died at the age of sixty-three on March 15, 1966. More than a year later, the Strongs would learn that the Potter Palmer Group had acquired the Globetrotters for $3,710,000. Prior to the sale, co-executors and a board of directors, which included Inman Jackson, operated the Globetrotters.

Around the time of the Globetrotters' acquisition by the Palmer Group, the *Chicago Sun-Times* ran a short story regarding Saperstein's estate that was valued at $2,422,335.[1]

"Yeah, old Abe Saperstein made a lot of money off of us blacks," said Alvin Spearman, now eighty-seven years old, living on Chicago's South Side.[2] Whether Ted Jr. expressed any resentment about the millions Saperstein earned from operating the Globetrotters remains unknown. Most insiders knew Saperstein liked Ted Jr. and would do whatever he could to help him when asked. Ted Jr. worked in Saperstein's Chicago office until the sale of the Globetrotters was finalized in 1968. In the early 1970s, he landed a clerk's position with the U.S. Post Office, and he lived in obscurity at 42nd and King Drive. Florence Faulkner divorced him in 1967.

On August 6, 1977, the *Chicago Defender* ran a story I wrote titled "A Tower of Strength: Theodore Strong, 83, Still an Active Leader." The article delighted Strong Sr., and while I was home from college during Christmas break, Strong Sr. called and said, "You need to talk to Ted. He'll talk to you." So, in late February 1978, Strong Sr. arranged a time for me to come to his house and meet and interview Ted Jr. The meeting never occurred. Ted Jr.'s health had begun to fail gradually by 1975. "Smoking and drinking got the best of him," Strong Sr. said, as Ted Jr. retired to his home at 4224 S. King Drive on the South Side.[3]

On the evening of March 1, 1978, Ted Jr. and other Chicagoans tolerated the 90-degree temperature that was common for the Midwestern city during that time of the year. He received a visit from a female friend, and they sat talking and watching television. Ted Jr.'s emphysema had a tendency to flare up, and this evening it gradually worsened as the night went on. The six-foot-six-inch former Negro Leagues and Globetrotter great began to heave mightily to catch his breath. Many times before he was able to recover and resume his conversations or laughter with friends and family. This night his friend sensed he wasn't recovering. She leaped from her chair and went out of the apartment to summon a neighbor. When she returned with the neighbor, they found Ted Jr. standing, coughing and wheezing, trying to catch his breath.

An ambulance was summoned, but when it arrived they found Ted Jr. on the floor with his friend and neighbors trying to comfort him. One of the neighbors called Ted Jr.'s brother Nathaniel, who lived a short distance from where Ted Jr. lived. The neighbor informed Nathaniel that his brother was being taken to Provident Hospital. By the time Nathaniel and Ted Jr.'s other siblings arrived at the hospital, the gentle giant, Mr. Hands, The Jeep was dead. Time of death was recorded as March 2, 1978, at 1:35 a.m. The death certificate shows the cause of death as "arteriosclerotic cardiovascular disease in association with pulmonary emphysema."

He had just celebrated his sixty-first birthday several months earlier, and even though he at times labored with the emphysema after retiring from sports, his passing came as a surprise. The *Chicago Tribune* columnist David Condon, in the March 4 edition, wrote a short blurb about Ted Jr. passing. On Sunday evening, March 5, friends, family, and those who remembered Ted Strong Jr. made their way to Carter Funeral Chapel at 2100 E. 75th Street to pay their respects. The following day he was buried in the first available plot in Lincoln Cemetery in Chicago. The cemetery representative offered the first available plot to those of limited financial means. Ted Jr. did not receive a military burial, and the grave was unmarked. In 2014, the Society for American Baseball Research (SABR) Negro Leagues Baseball Grave Marker Project Committee purchased a headstone to mark Ted Jr.'s grave.

Lincoln Cemetery, established in 1911, is also the final resting place for noted African Americans such as jazz musician Gene Ammons; Bessie Coleman, the first African American woman to gain a pilot's license; Robert S. Abbott, founder of the *Chicago Defender*; and ironically Andrew "Rube" Foster, founder of the Negro National League and Baseball Hall of Famer.

Strong Sr. never slowed in his devotion to uplifting his race. He and his longtime companion Ernestine finally married on September 30, 1965, in Chicago. They were blessed with ten children and remained on Chicago's South Side. Once a week, Strong Sr. would conduct in-home teaching sessions to his children about black history and metaphysics. Other childhood friends of the Strong children and I knew that on the evening of the teaching sessions our friends were unavailable. We were allowed to sit in on the sessions, but after one session, other childhood buddies and I had no clue of what Mr. Strong was putting down. So we stayed away and caught up with our friends the next day.

Strong Sr. never lost his love of baseball and religiously watched Sunday afternoon games on television. In 1975, he became a beat representative for the Chicago Police Department's Beat Representative Program. As a beat representative, Strong Sr. was responsible for serving as a liaison between the citizens in the neighborhood and the police officers assigned to that area. The program was designed by the Chicago Police Department to "reaffirm emphasis on the citizen's responsibility and role in crime prevention and to stimulate active citizen participation in crime prevention efforts."[4] Strong Sr. served as a member of the Beat Representative 2nd District steering committee. At that time, the steering committee helped police develop ways to combat crime in the 2nd District of Chicago.

"We [black people] must work together to combat problems in our communities. I hope young blacks understand this also," Strong said, pointing to some youngsters playing in the street in the neighborhood. "The future belongs to our young, but us older blacks must help our young prepare for their future today."[5]

For seven more years, Theodore Relighn Strong Sr. continued to vigorously struggle against the ravages of vices that would increasingly plague the African American community on Chicago's South Side. Drugs, prostitution, alcoholism, gangs—it didn't matter to Strong Sr. He had seen it all before, but now it seemed to increase at a rate that had even him shaking his head. He maintained that higher forces knew what was going on, and they profited from it.

At the age of ninety, after a short illness, the Reverend Theodore Relighn Strong Sr. died on February 19, 1984, at Mt. Sinai Hospital on Chicago's South Side. Several days later at the memorial service for Strong Sr., hundreds filed into Carter Funeral Chapel on the South Side. The Rev. Morris Gordon, Pastor of Parkway Gardens Christian Church, conducted the service. He spoke highly of the father of his childhood buddy Othello. His eulogy of the patriarch of the Strong family brought laughter to many and nods of agreement from those in attendance.

At Strong Sr.'s request, his body was cremated. He left to mourn his memory his wife Ernestine, nineteen children, twenty-nine grandchildren, and forty-three great-grandchildren. After the service, many in attendance paid their condolences to the family members, and stayed around to chat with old friends from the Negro Baseball Leagues who remembered "Pops" for his candor, honesty, and drive.

Othello Strong smiled and nodded as he listened to many of his friends talk about his father. He had retired after many years of service for Careful Cleaners. Several years before, Othello had been diagnosed with prostate cancer. He battled the disease until June 28, 1986, when he died with family and friends at his bedside at the Veterans Administration's Lakeside Medical Center in Chicago.

On July 5, 1986, a warm, sunny summer morning at Park Garden Christian Church, the Rev. Morris Gordon performed the service for his childhood buddy. Again, he spoke of the good times he and his buddy enjoyed as hundreds listened. "I handled it," Rev. Gordon said. "Othello's wife, Jackie, wouldn't leave the casket. Yes, we marched him off [to the grave site]," he added.[6] Othello's other buddies, Herbert Wooley and Ted "Double-Duty" Radcliffe, made remarks. Unfortunately, Alvin Spearman was unable to attend due to prior commitments. Mr. Spearman explained that his buddy had been ill for a long time and "as the end neared, I tried to keep my schedule open but it didn't work out. I loved my buddy. Othello was the reason I got into baseball and his brother Ted was the best all-around athlete I ever saw."[7]

Othello was buried in Burr Oak Cemetery in Alsip, Illinois, a suburb of Chicago. The SABR Negro Leagues Baseball Grave Marker Project Committee held a grave marking ceremony in June 2005.

EPILOGUE

It has been almost eighty years since Ted Strong Jr. burst onto the African American sports landscape. As a young African American living in the Black Belt of Chicago, he had dreams and aspirations of making it big in the sports he came to love. He realized his dreams but only in the African American sports world.

Who can know what Ted Jr. would have accomplished had race relations in America been based on a man's character instead of the color of his skin? He stood out among the best of the best in the Negro Baseball Leagues and with the Harlem Globetrotters. The African American press covered his feats and local newspapers in the cities where the Harlem Globetrotters played published the news releases and photographs that were fed to them by the Globetrotters' publicity team. He was one of the attractions that Abe Saperstein used to bring people out to see the Globetrotters and the man "with the biggest hands in basketball."

As he excelled in the African American sports world, it can be said that he exploded from the launch pad in the 1930s, hit the afterburners in the 1940s, but could not break into space by the 1950s. As a man, he knew he was as good or better than most of the white players he competed against. His hope of one day playing against the white boys in the "major leagues" was heightened so many times by white baseball team owners, but Father Time caught up to him and many of the Negro Leagues stars. When Ted Jr. finally decided that he might as well enjoy himself while he could, it was a familiar resound heard from many Negro Leagues players. Who could blame them?

As the effort to integrate baseball kept snagging on the web of racism, the call for African American pride and ownership increased. In 1942 veteran Negro Leagues manager Vic Harris said that he frowned upon getting African American players into the majors. He felt that African Americans should improve their own leagues and then challenge the white teams. Harris's call to "do for self" gained momentum in the African American community through the middle of the 1940s. With the end of World War II in September 1945, many of the stars of the Negro Leagues like Ted Jr. were returning home and rejoining their baseball teams. Research has shown that attendance at the Negro Leagues games consistently outdrew the white leagues. Coupled with the relentless demands of the Negro press and organizations, money and pressure were the primary reasons the white leagues, led by Brooklyn Dodger president and general manager Branch Rickey, seriously worked on the baseball integration question. He first tried it in 1945 when he attempted to launch another "Negro Leagues" owned by whites, but that effort collapsed when the cost proved to be too great. When Negro Leagues sportswriter Wendell Smith again pushed the names of Negro Leagues players who should be considered to break the color barrier, Rickey finally gave serious consideration and the rest, as they say, is history.

Ted Jr. didn't get his shot at playing in the white leagues because he wasn't of the temperament that was needed at the time. Ted Jr. wouldn't have taken what Jackie Robinson took when he joined the Dodgers farm and big-league teams. Yes, Ted Jr. played with the Globetrotters in all-white, small-town America for a number of years, but an "eye for an eye and a tooth for a tooth" had been taught to him by Strong Sr.

People have asked me why Ted Jr. isn't in the Baseball or Basketball Hall of Fame. I can only say that his baseball and basketball feats were overshadowed by the feats of others who honestly deserved recognition such as Satchel Paige, Josh Gibson, Cool Papa Bell, Marcus Haynes, and Goose Tatum. Not that those mentioned above have received their due, it is time for us to uncover other unsung heroes, despite their human flaws, and tell their stories. Lovers of baseball want to know more about men like Ted Strong Jr. Other authors have paved the way for myself and others to uncover the stories of Negro Leagues baseball and basketball pioneers like Ted Jr. This book tells you about the life of Theodore Relighn Strong Jr. and his accomplishments in baseball and basketball. It has been my regret for decades not having had the opportunity to interview Ted Jr. My goodness, the stories he could have told about Negro Leagues players and Globetrotter hoopsters. He lived a life unlike any other and only by sitting down and probing him for details and his opinions about situations and what he experienced would we all have obtained a better understanding of the trials and tribulations he endured. Fate had other plans for me and him, and I guess what you are reading now is what I was destined to share with the world about him.

I hope those of you who are reading this book and know of someone who has had a storied life will grab your tape recorder and sit down and ask questions of that person. They are probably just waiting on someone to show an interest in them and with a question or two you could probably get a wealth of information that will fascinate you. Now, you might be saying to yourself, "I am not a writer." Who said you needed to write a book? You can use your computer and write down the person's life story, print it, and save it for future generations to discover. Libraries across this country have research collections and genealogy departments that might be willing to accept your donation of the person's life story especially if that person was a champion in the community.

Ted Strong Jr. undoubtedly fits that criteria. He paved the way for Meadowlark Lemon, Curley Neal, Jackie Robinson, Willie Mays, and countless others who graced the American sports landscape. We owe it to ourselves to research harder, pick the brains of those still among the living, and write the stories of people who lived extraordinary lives. If America is to become an even greater nation, we must uncover the stories of these Americans. With today's technology of smartphones that can record audio and capture video in an instant, we should be able to document people from the 1960s and 1970s who made a difference in their communities. Just imagine what gems we could have captured with today's technology when Ted Jr. roamed the baseball diamonds and hardwood courts.

APPENDIX A:
FACTS ABOUT TED STRONG JR.

BASEBALL

- Ted Strong Jr. played in seven Negro Leagues Baseball East-West All-Star Games. In 1939 he received 508,327 votes, the most in all of black baseball history.
- In 1940, Ted Jr. played in the Mexican League and finished second in slugging percentage behind Cool Papa Bell and was also second to Bell in triples (only one behind the legendary speedster). He had eleven home runs, tying Josh Gibson for second, one behind Bell.
- In 1946, the switch-hitting power hitter captured the home run crown of the Negro American League.
- Ted Jr. was the leading hitter for right fielders averaging .500 with a slugging percentage of .609.
- Ted Jr. was one of the tallest players in East-West All-Star Classics, six feet, six inches.

BASKETBALL

- Ted Jr. was a key member of the 1940 Harlem Globetrotter basketball team that won the World Professional Basketball Championship.
- Ted Jr. played in the historic 1948 game where the Globetrotters defeated the all-white Minneapolis Lakers anchored by the legendary center George Mikan.
- Ted Jr. had the nicknames of "The Jeep" and "Mr. Hands."

APPENDIX B:
QUOTES ABOUT TED STRONG JR.

Ted Strong . . . was our shortstop, maybe the tallest shortstop ever to play the game. He was darn near seven feet tall, a switch-hitter with tremendous power—I saw him hit mammoth home runs from both sides of the plate in one game. Ted was like Cal Ripken, only bigger. They put him at short because he had great hands and a rifle arm. In fact, he was one of the first real tall guys who could do a lot of things. Now, of course, tall guys are all slick just like he was, but back then it was a shock.
—**John "Buck" O'Neil**, first baseman, Kansas City Monarchs, *I Was Right On Time* by Buck O'Neil, pages 86–87

Ted should have played in the majors. He was truly one of the greatest athletes I've ever seen, although, truth be told, he might have been better if he wasn't so easily led astray. Ted was the type of guy who, if I came down and met him in the hotel lobby and said, 'Come on, Ted, let's go to church,' he'd want to go. But somebody could beat me down there and say, 'Let's go to this dive down the street and drink all night,' and he'd be all for it. That was Ted—he'd blow either way.
—**John "Buck" O'Neil**, first baseman, Kansas City Monarchs, *I Was Right On Time* by Buck O'Neil, page 87

In 1942 . . . we had a tremendous ball club that year. A lot of the boys had jumped to Mexico, and they all came back in '42. . . . Ted Strong was just as good a ballplayer as there was in baseball, but he kind of laid on the bottle. That got him in his late years.
—**Hilton Smith**, pitcher, Kansas City Monarchs, *Voices from the Great Black Baseball Leagues* by John Holway, page 290

We always thought that Ted Strong was about the most ideal ballplayer. Had all the tools. A switch hitter and could play just about anywhere. Anywhere you put Ted, Ted was at home—first base, shortstop, outfield. From outfield he could really throw; you couldn't take a turn from first to third on him. He wound up in the Texas League as [Willard] Brown did. Getting old, fat, out of shape, but he was up around the home run leaders in the Texas League.

—**Othello Renfroe**, Kansas City Monarchs, *Voices from the Great Black Baseball Leagues* by John Holway, page 345

A trace of nonprofessionalism also cropped out here and there yesterday when fielders took throws or line drives with one hand when two would have been safer. Strong, the tall, magnificently proportioned first baseman from the Indianapolis ABCs, insists on "show-boating" with his glove, a trick of vainglory which he should forget even if one of his hands is as large as the average man's two. (He is a sensational basketball player of [*sic*] wintertimes.)

—**Lloyd Lewis**, journalist, *Chicago Daily News*, "'Negro Ball Is Faster' Says Lloyd Lewis," *Chicago Daily News*, August 27, 1938, page 8

[Jackie Robinson] was some ballplayer. I won't say he was the best ballplayer we had in those days but he was adequate and we were all proud of him. Monte Irvin, Willie Wells, Ted Strong—they were all better than Jackie.

—**Ted "Double Duty" Radcliffe**, player and manager, Negro Leagues, *Ted "Double Duty" Radcliffe: 36 Years of Pitching & Catching in Baseball's Negro Leagues* by Kyle P. McNary, page 183

All of our other outfielders could throw the ball. Ted Strong, who played several seasons with the Monarchs, had a powerful arm. Having Ted in right field helped make up for having Willard Brown in center.

—**Frazier "Slow" Robinson**, catcher, Negro Leagues, *Catching Dreams: My Life in the Negro Baseball Leagues* by Frazier Robinson and Paul Bauer, page 56

Nobody made the kind of money Satchel made, but there were still guys who could run through money like Satchel. You had Ted Strong, you had one of Newark's pitchers, Terris McDuffie, you had a bunch of guys wouldn't save their money. They'd just go on. They figured they'd have some fun. Ted Strong also played basketball with the Globetrotters. He was a very good athlete. There wasn't no telling how good he would have been if he'd have just played baseball and stayed away from that bottle. That's where all his money went. Once, before the war, Strong was at the All-Star Game, and they were looking for him to put him in the lineup. When they went to his hotel he was laying up there in bed—dead drunk. They had to put him in a bathtub to try to sober him up. He'd just stay in them nightclubs and drink. He had a good voice. He liked to sing. He just messed up like that. He spent a lot of his money.

—**Frazier "Slow" Robinson**, catcher, Negro Leagues, *Catching Dreams: My Life in the Negro Baseball Leagues* by Frazier Robinson and Paul Bauer, page 75

I'm gonna tell you, there was a ballplayer named Ted Strong, but he was a wasted product. What a ballplayer! He could do everything. He could hit from both sides, great arm, great speed, power, hit percentage-wise, but he wouldn't take care of himself. He drank, stayed out at night. He just did everything off natural ability. He was never really in shape. If he had taken better care of himself I think he would have been better than all of them.

—**Sherwood Brewer**, outfielder and shortstop, Negro Leagues, "Pitch Black" by Kyle McNary, www.pitchblackbaseball.com, 2004

The new Globe Trotter players were bigger, faster, stronger, and more athletic than their predecessors. Some of them had *true* college experience, as opposed to the faux college pedigrees that Abe had made up. The new players included: Ted Strong, a six-foot-three, 207-pound bruiser from Baltimore with gigantic meat hooks ("The biggest hands in basketball," Abe would say), who was also an All-Star first baseman for Abe's Chicago American Giants; Babe Pressley from Cleveland, a terrific rebounder and defenseman; Bernie Price, a six-four center from Toledo; Zach Clayton, a Philadelphia native with a linebacker's physique; and Bill Ford, from Columbus, Ohio, a smooth outside shooter. . . .

In addition to the craps shooting, Abe had added another troubling bit to the show: Ted Strong spent the entire game chattering in a high-pitched, childlike, almost unintelligible voice—what one reporter described as "forty minutes of vociferous squealing by big Ted Strong, the gigantic guard, [who] drew gales of laughter with his moans of 'foul, foul.'"

—*Spinning the Globe: The Rise, Fall and Return to Greatness of the Harlem Globetrotters* by Ben Green, pages 97 and 101

APPENDIX C: TED STRONG JR.'S BASEBALL STATISTICS

TED STRONG, JR. NEGRO LEAGUES STATISTICS
(COMPILED BY NOIRTECH RESEARCH, INC.)

Year	Game Date	DH	Team	AB	RN	Hits	Dbl.	Trp.	HR	RBI	SAC	W	SB	ER	Opp. Team	Site	Avg.
1937	Saturday, May 08, 1937	1	Indianapolis Athletics	4	0	0	0	0	0	0	0	0	0	0	SLS	1	
1937	Saturday, May 08, 1937	2	Indianapolis Athletics	4	2	3	1	1	0	2	0	1	0	0	SLS	1	
1937	Sunday, May 16, 1937	2	Indianapolis Athletics	2	0	0	0	0	0	0	0	1	0	0	MRS	2	
1937	Sunday, May 23, 1937	1	Indianapolis Athletics	3	0	0	0	0	0	0	0	1	0	0	DTS	2	
1937	Sunday, May 23, 1937	2	Indianapolis Athletics	4	1	1	0	0	0	0	0	1	0	0	DTS	2	
1937	Saturday, May 29, 1937		Indianapolis Athletics	3	2	2	0	0	0	0	0	2	0	0	CCT	1	
1937	Sunday, May 30, 1937		Indianapolis Athletics	4	1	2	1	0	0	0	0	0	0	0	CCT	1	
1937	Monday, July 05, 1937	1	Indianapolis Athletics	3	1	1	0	0	0	1	0	2	0	1	BBB	2	
1937	Monday, July 05, 1937	2	Indianapolis Athletics	3	0	1	0	0	0	0	0	1	1	2	BBB	2	
1937	Saturday, July 10, 1937		Indianapolis Athletics	4	0	0	0	0	0	0	0	0	0	0	CAG	2	
1937	Sunday, July 11, 1937	2	Indianapolis Athletics	5	2	2	0	0	0	0	0	0	0	1	CAG	2	
1937	Sunday, August 08, 1937		Indianapolis Athletics	4	1	2	0	0	1	2	0	0	0	2	EAS	3	
1937	Sunday, August 29, 1937		Kansas City Monarchs	5	1	2	2	0	0	0	0	0	0	0	TRU	3	

Year	Date	G	Team	AB	R	H	2B	3B	HR	RBI	SB	PO	A	E	Code	No.
1937	Monday, September 06, 1937	2	Kansas City Monarchs	3	0	0	0	0	0	0	0	0	0	0	CCT	1
1937	Wednesday, September 08, 1937	1	Kansas City Monarchs	3	1	1	0	0	0	0	0	1	0	0	CAG	3
1937	Sunday, September 12, 1937	2	Kansas City Monarchs	5	1	2	0	0	0	1	0	2	0	0	CAG	2
1937	Monday, September 13, 1937	3	Kansas City Monarchs	4	1	2	1	0	1	0	0	0	0	0	CAG	3
1937	Friday, September 17, 1937	6	Kansas City Monarchs	3	0	1	0	0	0	0	0	0	0	1	CAG	1
1937	Sunday, September 19, 1937		Chicago American Giants	3	2	0	0	0	0	0	0	2	0	2	HSG	3
1937	Sunday, September 26, 1937		Chicago American Giants	5	3	4	1	1	0	4	0	2	0	0	HSG	3
1937	Wednesday, October 06, 1937		Kansas City Monarchs	4	1	1	0	0	0	0	0	1	0	0	MLA	3
1937 Count				**78**	**20**	**26**	**6**	**1**	**2**	**11**	**0**	**16**	**1**	**9**		**.333**
1938	Sunday, April 10, 1938		Kansas City Monarchs	4	1	4	0	0	0	0	0	0	0	0	PDS	3
1938	Sunday, May 15, 1938	1	Indianapolis ABC's	3	0	0	0	0	0	0	0	0	0	0	MRS	2
1938	Sunday, May 22, 1938	1	Indianapolis ABC's	3	0	2	0	0	0	0	0	0	0	0	KCM	2
1938	Sunday, May 22, 1938	2	Indianapolis ABC's	3	0	0	0	0	0	0	0	0	0	0	KCM	2
1938	Sunday, May 29, 1938	1	Indianapolis ABC's	5	2	3	2	0	0	0	0	0	0	0	BBB	1

(continued)

Year	Game Date	DH	Team	AB	RN	Hits	Dbl.	Trp.	HR	RBI	SAC	W	SB	ER	Opp. Team	Site	Avg.
1938	Friday, June 10, 1938		Indianapolis ABC's	3	1	0	0	0	0	0	0	1	1	0	BCA	2	
1938	Sunday, June 12, 1938	1	Indianapolis ABC's	5	0	2	0	0	0	0	0	0	1	0	BCA	2	
1938	Sunday, June 12, 1938	2	Indianapolis ABC's	2	1	1	0	0	0	0	0	0	0	0	BCA	2	
1938	Tuesday, June 14, 1938		Indianapolis ABC's	3	1	0	0	0	0	0	0	1	0	0	BCA	2	
1938	Sunday, July 10, 1938	1	Indianapolis ABC's	4	0	1	0	0	0	0	0	0	1	0	BCA	2	
1938	Sunday, July 10, 1938	2	Indianapolis ABC's	3	1	1	0	0	0	2	0	0	0	0	BCA	2	
1938	Monday, July 11, 1938		Indianapolis ABC's	4	2	2	0	0	0	1	0	0	0	0	BCA	3	
1938	Monday, July 25, 1938		Indianapolis ABC's	2	0	0	0	0	0	1	0	2	1	0	BBB	3	
1938	Saturday, August 06, 1938		Indianapolis ABC's	5	3	5	1	1	0	3	0	0	2	0	CAG	2	
1938	Sunday, August 07, 1938	1	Indianapolis ABC's	3	1	2	0	0	0	1	0	1	0	0	CAG	2	
1938	Sunday, August 14, 1938	1	Indianapolis ABC's	4	0	1	1	0	0	0	0	0	0	0	KCM	2	
1938	Sunday, August 14, 1938	2	Indianapolis ABC's	2	0	0	0	0	0	0	0	1	0	0	KCM	2	
1938	Sunday, August 21, 1938		Indianapolis ABC's	3	1	0	0	0	0	0	0	1	0	0	EAS	3	
1938 Count				**61**	**14**	**24**	**4**	**1**	**0**	**8**	**0**	**7**	**6**	**0**			**.393**

1939		Date		Team												
1939	1	Sunday, May 14, 1939	Kansas City Monarchs	3	2	2	1	0	1	2	0	1	0	0	MRS	1
1939	2	Sunday, May 14, 1939	Kansas City Monarchs	2	0	1	0	0	0	0	0	1	0	0	MRS	1
1939		Monday, May 15, 1939	Kansas City Monarchs	5	0	0	0	0	0	0	0	0	0	0	MRS	3
1939		Saturday, May 20, 1939	Kansas City Monarchs	3	0	1	0	0	0	0	0	1	0	2	CAG	2
1939		Sunday, May 21, 1939	Kansas City Monarchs	4	1	1	0	0	0	0	0	0	1	1	CAG	2
1939		Monday, May 22, 1939	Kansas City Monarchs	4	1	0	0	0	0	0	1	1	0	1	CAG	2
1939	1	Sunday, May 28, 1939	Kansas City Monarchs	2	1	1	0	0	0	0	0	1	1	0	ABC	1
1939	2	Sunday, May 28, 1939	Kansas City Monarchs	3	1	1	0	0	0	0	0	1	1	0	ABC	1
1939	1	Monday, May 29, 1939	Kansas City Monarchs	3	0	0	0	0	0	0	1	0	0	0	CBR	1
1939	2	Monday, May 29, 1939	Kansas City Monarchs	2	1	1	1	0	0	3	0	1	0	0	CBR	1
1939	1	Sunday, June 04, 1939	Kansas City Monarchs	3	2	1	0	1	0	0	0	1	2	0	SLS	1
1939	2	Sunday, June 04, 1939	Kansas City Monarchs	2	0	1	0	0	0	0	0	1	0	0	SLS	1
1939	1	Sunday, June 11, 1939	Kansas City Monarchs	3	1	0	0	0	0	0	0	1	0	0	MRS	3
1939	2	Sunday, June 11, 1939	Kansas City Monarchs	4	1	1	0	0	0	0	0	0	0	0	MRS	3
1939	1	Sunday, July 02, 1939	Kansas City Monarchs	5	0	1	0	0	0	0	0	0	0	0	CAG	1
1939	2	Sunday, July 02, 1939	Kansas City Monarchs	2	0	0	0	0	0	0	0	0	0	0	CAG	1

(continued)

Year	Game Date	DH	Team	AB	RN	Hits	Dbl.	Trp.	HR	RBI	SAC	W	SB	ER	Opp. Team	Site	Avg.
1939	Sunday, July 09, 1939	1	Kansas City Monarchs	4	0	0	0	0	0	0	0	0	0	0	SLS	1	
1939	Sunday, July 09, 1939	2	Kansas City Monarchs	3	0	1	0	0	0	0	0	0	0	0	SLS	1	
1939	Sunday, July 23, 1939		Kansas City Monarchs	4	1	2	0	0	0	1	1	0	1	0	CAG	3	
1939	Saturday, July 29, 1939		Kansas City Monarchs	3	1	1	0	0	0	0	0	1	1	0	CAG	2	
1939	Sunday, July 30, 1939	1	Kansas City Monarchs	4	2	1	1	0	0	2	0	0	3	0	CAG	2	
1939	Saturday, August 12, 1939		Kansas City Monarchs	4	0	2	0	0	0	1	0	1	1	0	MRS	2	
1939	Sunday, August 20, 1939	1	Kansas City Monarchs	4	0	1	0	0	0	0	0	0	0	0	MRS	1	
1939	Sunday, August 20, 1939	2	Kansas City Monarchs	3	0	0	0	0	0	0	0	0	0	1	MRS	1	
1939	Thursday, August 31, 1939		Kansas City Monarchs	4	0	2	1	0	0	1	0	0	0	0	SLS	3	
1939	Friday, September 01, 1939		Kansas City Monarchs	4	0	1	0	0	0	0	0	0	1	0	SLS	3	
1939	Sunday, September 03, 1939	1	Kansas City Monarchs	4	0	1	0	0	0	0	0	0	0	0	SLS	1	
1939	Sunday, September 03, 1939	2	Kansas City Monarchs	3	0	0	0	0	0	0	0	0	0	0	SLS	1	
1939	Monday, September 04, 1939	3	Kansas City Monarchs	4	0	1	0	0	0	0	0	0	0	1	SLS	1	
1939 Count				**98**	**15**	**25**	**4**	**1**	**1**	**11**	**3**	**12**	**12**	**7**			**.255**

1941	Sunday, May 18, 1941		Kansas City Monarchs	3	0	1	0	0	0	0	1	0	CAG	2
1941	Sunday, May 25, 1941	1	Kansas City Monarchs	4	1	2	0	1	3	1	0	0	MRS	1
1941	Sunday, June 01, 1941	1	Kansas City Monarchs	4	1	0	0	0	0	0	1	0	JRC	1
1941	Saturday, June 14, 1941		Kansas City Monarchs	3	1	0	0	0	0	0	1	0	CAG	3
1941	Sunday, June 29, 1941	1	Kansas City Monarchs	4	1	1	0	0	0	0	0	0	NBY	1
1941	Monday, June 30, 1941		Kansas City Monarchs	4	0	0	0	0	0	0	0	0	NBY	1
1941	Friday, July 04, 1941	1	Kansas City Monarchs	3	2	2	1	0	2	0	2	0	CAG	3
1941	Sunday, July 06, 1941	1	Kansas City Monarchs	3	0	1	0	0	0	0	0	0	CAG	1
1941	Sunday, July 06, 1941	2	Kansas City Monarchs	2	0	1	0	0	0	0	1	0	CAG	1
1941	Monday, July 07, 1941		Kansas City Monarchs	4	1	2	1	1	2	1	1	1	CAG	1
1941	Sunday, July 13, 1941	1	Kansas City Monarchs	3	1	1	0	0	1	0	1	0	BBB	1
1941	Sunday, July 13, 1941	2	Kansas City Monarchs	3	1	1	0	1	2	1	0	0	BBB	1
1941	Thursday, July 17, 1941		Kansas City Monarchs	3	0	1	0	0	1	0	2	0	PDS	2
1941	Saturday, July 19, 1941	1	Kansas City Monarchs	5	1	0	0	0	2	0	0	0	PDS	2
1941	Saturday, July 19, 1941	2	Kansas City Monarchs	2	0	0	0	0	0	0	1	0	PDS	2

(continued)

Year	Game Date	DH	Team	AB	RN	Hits	Dbl.	Trp.	HR	RBI	SAC	W	SB	ER	Opp. Team	Site	Avg.
1941	Sunday, July 20, 1941	1	Kansas City Monarchs	4	2	2	0	0	0	0	0	1	0	0	NYC	3	
1941	Sunday, July 27, 1941		Kansas City Monarchs	4	1	2	1	1	0	1	0	0	0	0	EAS	3	
1941	Sunday, August 03, 1941	1	Kansas City Monarchs	3	2	1	0	0	1	1	0	2	0	0	NSS	3	
1941	Sunday, August 03, 1941	2	Kansas City Monarchs	4	0	2	0	0	0	1	0	0	0	0	NSS	3	
1941	Sunday, August 10, 1941	1	Kansas City Monarchs	3	0	0	0	0	0	0	0	1	0	0	NSS	1	
1941	Sunday, August 10, 1941	2	Kansas City Monarchs	2	1	1	0	0	0	1	0	2	0	0	NSS	1	
1941	Sunday, August 17, 1941	1	Kansas City Monarchs	4	1	2	2	0	0	1	0	0	0	0	BEG	1	
1941	Sunday, August 17, 1941	2	Kansas City Monarchs	3	2	0	0	0	0	0	0	1	0	0	BEG	1	
1941	Sunday, August 24, 1941	1	Kansas City Monarchs	4	1	2	0	0	0	0	0	1	1	0	NWE	3	
1941	Sunday, September 21, 1941	1	Kansas City Monarchs	4	3	2	0	0	0	1	0	1	0	0	CCC	1	
1941	Sunday, September 21, 1941	2	Kansas City Monarchs	3	0	0	0	0	0	0	0	0	0	0	CCC	1	
1941 Count				**88**	**23**	**27**	**4**	**2**	**3**	**19**	**2**	**20**	**1**	**1**			**.307**
1942	Sunday, May 10, 1942	1	Kansas City Monarchs	3	0	1	0	0	0	1	0	1	0	0	CAG	2	
1942	Sunday, May 10, 1942	2	Kansas City Monarchs	3	1	1	0	0	0	0	0	1	0	0	CAG	2	

Year	Date	G	Team										Opp	
1942	Sunday, May 17, 1942	1	Kansas City Monarchs	3	1	1	0	0	0	0	1	0	MRS	1
1942	Sunday, May 24, 1942	1	Chicago Brown Bombers	4	0	1	0	0	0	0	0	0	CCC	2
1942	Saturday, May 30, 1942	1	Kansas City Monarchs	4	1	1	0	0	0	0	1	0	CAG	1
1942	Saturday, May 30, 1942	2	Kansas City Monarchs	3	2	2	0	0	0	0	1	0	CAG	1
1942	Sunday, May 31, 1942	1	Kansas City Monarchs	4	1	3	0	1	0	0	0	0	BBB	1
1942	Sunday, May 31, 1942	2	Kansas City Monarchs	1	0	0	0	0	0	0	0	0	BBB	1
1942	Sunday, June 07, 1942	1	Kansas City Monarchs	4	0	0	0	0	0	0	1	0	BBB	2
1942	Sunday, June 07, 1942	2	Kansas City Monarchs	4	1	3	0	1	1	0	0	0	BBB	2
1942	Sunday, June 14, 1942	1	Kansas City Monarchs	3	0	1	1	0	0	0	0	0	CBE	2
1942	Wednesday, June 17, 1942		Kansas City Monarchs	5	2	2	2	0	1	0	0	0	BEG	2
1942	Thursday, June 18, 1942		Kansas City Monarchs	4	0	1	0	0	0	0	0	0	HSG	2
1942	Friday, June 21, 1942		Kansas City Monarchs	4	1	1	0	0	0	0	0	0	MRS	1
1942	Friday, June 26, 1942		Kansas City Monarchs	3	0	1	0	0	1	0	1	0	BBB	3
1942	Sunday, June 28, 1942		Kansas City Monarchs	5	2	2	0	0	1	0	2	0	CAG	3
1942	Saturday, July 04, 1942	1	Kansas City Monarchs	4	1	0	0	0	0	0	1	0	MRS	2

(continued)

Year	Game Date	DH	Team	AB	RN	Hits	Dbl.	Trp.	HR	RBI	SAC	W	SB	ER	Opp. Team	Site	Avg.
1942	Sunday, July 05, 1942	1	Kansas City Monarchs	5	2	2	0	0	1	3	0	0	0	0	BBB	2	
1942	Sunday, July 05, 1942	2	Kansas City Monarchs	3	1	0	0	0	0	0	0	0	0	0	BBB	2	
1942	Sunday, July 19, 1942	1	Kansas City Monarchs	5	2	3	0	0	0	2	0	0	0	0	CAG	2	
1942	Tuesday, July 21, 1942		Kansas City Monarchs	4	0	1	0	0	0	0	0	1	1	0	HSG	2	
1942	Sunday, July 26, 1942	1	Kansas City Monarchs	5	0	3	0	0	0	1	0	0	0	0	MRS	3	
1942	Sunday, July 26, 1942	2	Kansas City Monarchs	3	1	0	0	0	0	1	1	1	0	0	MRS	3	
1942	Sunday, August 02, 1942	2	Kansas City Monarchs	4	2	3	2	0	0	2	0	0	0	0	NYC	3	
1942	Thursday, August 06, 1942		Kansas City Monarchs	5	0	1	0	0	0	1	0	0	0	0	PDS	2	
1942	Thursday, August 13, 1942		Kansas City Monarchs	5	1	0	0	0	0	0	1	0	0	0	HSG	2	
1942	Sunday, August 16, 1942		Kansas City Monarchs	3	0	1	0	0	0	0	0	1	0	0	EAS	3	
1942	Tuesday, August 18, 1942		Kansas City Monarchs	3	0	2	0	0	0	0	0	0	0	1	EAS	3	
1942	Sunday, August 23, 1942	1	Kansas City Monarchs	6	1	1	0	0	1	2	0	0	0	0	CAG	1	
1942	Sunday, August 23, 1942	2	Kansas City Monarchs	2	1	1	0	0	0	0	0	1	0	0	CAG	1	
1942	Sunday, August 30, 1942	1	Kansas City Monarchs	5	2	4	0	0	1	3	0	0	0	0	PDS	3	

Year	#	Date	Team												Opp	
1942		Tuesday, September 08, 1942	Kansas City Monarchs	5	1	1	0	0	0	0	0	0	0	0	HSG	2
1942	1	Thursday, September 10, 1942	Kansas City Monarchs	5	2	2	1	0	0	0	0	0	0	0	HSG	3
1942	2	Sunday, September 13, 1942	Kansas City Monarchs	3	1	2	0	0	1	0	0	1	0	0	HSG	3
1942	3	Sunday, September 13, 1942	Kansas City Monarchs	4	1	2	0	1	0	3	0	0	0	0	HSG	3
1942	4	Sunday, September 20, 1942	Kansas City Monarchs	4	0	0	0	0	0	0	0	0	0	0	HSG	1
1942	5	Tuesday, September 29, 1942	Kansas City Monarchs	5	2	1	0	0	0	0	2	1	1	0	HSG	3
1942 Count				**145**	**33**	**50**	**7**	**0**	**5**	**25**	**2**	**17**	**2**	**1**		**.345**
1946		Thursday, May 02, 1946	Kansas City Monarchs	4	1	0	0	0	0	0	0	1	0	2	INC	3
1946	1	Sunday, May 05, 1946	Kansas City Monarchs	4	0	0	0	0	0	0	0	0	0	0	CAG	2
1946		Tuesday, May 07, 1946	Kansas City Monarchs	4	3	3	0	0	0	4	0	1	0	0	CAG	3
1946		Sunday, May 12, 1946	Kansas City Monarchs	4	1	1	0	0	0	0	0	1	1	0	MRS	1
1946	1	Sunday, June 16, 1946	Kansas City Monarchs	4	3	3	1	0	0	2	0	0	0	0	CBE	1
1946		Sunday, June 30, 1946	Kansas City Monarchs	4	1	2	0	1	1	2	0	0	0	1	BBB	1
1946	1	Sunday, June 30, 1946	Kansas City Monarchs	3	2	2	0	0	0	2	0	0	0	0	BBB	1
1946	2	Tuesday, July 16, 1946	Kansas City Monarchs	4	0	1	0	0	0	0	0	0	0	0	NWE	2

(continued)

Year	Game Date	DH	Team	AB	RN	Hits	Dbl.	Trp.	HR	RBI	SAC	W	SB	ER	Opp. Team	Site	Avg.
1946	Sunday, July 21, 1946	1	Kansas City Monarchs	4	1	0	0	0	0	0	0	1	0	0	INC	1	
1946	Sunday, July 21, 1946	2	Kansas City Monarchs	4	0	0	0	0	0	0	0	0	0	0	INC	1	
1946	Tuesday, July 30, 1946		Kansas City Monarchs	5	1	2	1	0	0	3	0	0	0	0	INC	3	
1946	Sunday, August 04, 1946	1	Kansas City Monarchs	4	0	0	0	0	0	0	0	0	0	1	HSG	2	
1946	Sunday, August 04, 1946	2	Kansas City Monarchs	3	0	1	1	0	0	0	0	0	0	0	HSG	2	
1946	Tuesday, August 06, 1946		Kansas City Monarchs	3	0	0	0	0	0	0	0	1	0	0	NWE	2	
1946	Sunday, August 11, 1946	1	Kansas City Monarchs	3	0	0	0	0	0	0	0	1	0	0	CAG	1	
1946	Sunday, August 18, 1946	1	Kansas City Monarchs	3	2	1	0	0	0	0	0	2	0	0	MRS	1	
1946	Tuesday, August 27, 1946	1	Kansas City Monarchs	2	1	0	0	0	0	0	0	2	0	0	MRS	1	
1946	Sunday, September 01, 1946	1	Kansas City Monarchs	3	0	2	0	0	0	2	0	1	0	0	INC	1	
1946	Sunday, September 01, 1946	2	Kansas City Monarchs	1	1	1	0	0	0	0	0	2	0	0	INC	1	
1946	Tuesday, September 17, 1946	1	Kansas City Monarchs	4	0	1	0	0	0	1	0	0	0	0	NWE	3	
1946	Thursday, September 19, 1946	2	Kansas City Monarchs	3	1	0	0	0	0	0	0	1	0	0	NWE	2	
1946	Monday, September 23, 1946	3	Kansas City Monarchs	5	1	1	0	0	1	2	0	0	0	0	NWE	1	

Year	Date		Kansas City Monarchs													
1946	Tuesday, September 24, 1946	4	Kansas City Monarchs	3	0	0	0	0	0	0	0	0	0	NWE	1	.259
1946 Count				81	19	21	2	2	18	0	13	1	4			
1947	Sunday, May 25, 1947	1	Kansas City Monarchs	4	0	0	0	0	0	0	1	0	0	MRS	1	
1947	Tuesday, June 03, 1947		Kansas City Monarchs	3	0	0	0	0	0	0	1	0	0	CBE	3	
1947	Thursday, June 05, 1947	1	Kansas City Monarchs	0	0	0	0	0	0	0	1	0	0	CBE	1	
1947	Sunday, June 08, 1947	1	Kansas City Monarchs	4	0	2	1	0	2	0	0	0	0	INC	1	
1947	Sunday, June 08, 1947	2	Kansas City Monarchs	3	1	2	0	0	3	0	0	0	0	INC	1	
1947	Monday, June 16, 1947		Kansas City Monarchs	1	0	0	0	0	0	0	1	0	0	INC	1	
1947	Friday, June 20, 1947		Kansas City Monarchs	3	0	0	0	0	0	0	0	0	0	MRS	3	
1947	Friday, June 27, 1947	1	Kansas City Monarchs	1	0	1	1	0	0	0	0	0	0	MRS	1	
1947	Friday, July 04, 1947		Kansas City Monarchs	1	0	0	0	0	0	0	0	0	0	INC	3	
1947	Sunday, July 06, 1947	2	Kansas City Monarchs	4	0	0	0	0	0	0	0	0	0	NYC	2	
1947	Sunday, July 13, 1947	1	Kansas City Monarchs	3	0	2	0	0	0	0	1	0	0	BBB	1	
1947	Sunday, July 13, 1947	2	Kansas City Monarchs	0	2	0	0	0	0	0	0	0	2	BBB	1	
1947	Wednesday, August 06, 1947	2	Kansas City Monarchs	4	2	3	0	1	1	0	0	0	0	BBW	2	

(continued)

Year	Game Date	DH	Team	AB	RN	Hits	Dbl.	Trp.	HR	RBI	SAC	W	SB	ER	Opp. Team	Site	Avg.
1947	Sunday, August 10, 1947	2	Kansas City Monarchs	3	0	1	0	0	0	0	0	0	0	0	HSG	2	
1947 Count				**34**	**3**	**11**	**2**	**0**	**2**	**6**	**0**	**5**	**0**	**2**			**.324**
1948	Sunday, May 16, 1948	1	Indianapolis Clowns	2	0	2	0	0	0	0	0	2	0	0	BBB	2	
1948	Sunday, May 16, 1948	2	Indianapolis Clowns	3	1	2	0	0	0	0	0	0	0	1	BBB	2	
1948	Tuesday, May 18, 1948		Indianapolis Clowns	3	0	0	0	0	0	0	0	1	0	0	BBB	2	
1948	Sunday, May 23, 1948	2	Indianapolis Clowns	3	1	1	0	0	0	1	0	0	0	0	KCM	2	
1948	Tuesday, May 25, 1948		Indianapolis Clowns	3	2	2	0	0	0	2	0	1	0	0	KCM	3	
1948	Sunday, May 30, 1948		Indianapolis Clowns	2	0	0	0	0	0	0	1	2	0	0	KCM	3	
1948	Sunday, June 27, 1948	1	Indianapolis Clowns	3	0	0	0	0	0	0	0	1	0	0	BBB	2	
1948	Sunday, June 27, 1948	2	Indianapolis Clowns	1	0	1	0	0	0	1	0	0	0	0	BBB	2	
1948 Count				**20**	**4**	**8**	**0**	**0**	**0**	**4**	**1**	**7**	**0**	**1**			**.400**
Grand Count				605	131	192	29	7	15	102	8	97	23	25			.317

Legend: DH: Doubleheader; AB: At Bat; RN: Run; HITS: Hits; DBL: Double; TRP: Triple; HR: Home Run; RBI: Runs Batted In; SAC: Sacrifice; W: Walks; SB: Stolen Base; ER: Error; OPP TEAM: Opposing Team; SITE: Stadium Location

Legend for Stadiums of Opposing Teams: ABC: Indianapolis ABCs; BBB: Birmingham Black Barons; BCA: Atlanta Black Crackers; BEG: Baltimore Elite Giants; CAG: Chicago American Giants; CBE: Cleveland Buckeyes; CBR: Cleveland Bears; CCC: Cincinnati Clowns; CCT: Cincinnati Tigers; DTS: Detroit Stars; ETH: Ethiopian Clowns; HSG: Homestead Grays; INC: Indianapolis Clowns; JRC: Jacksonville Red Caps; MEC: Miami Ethiopian Clowns; MRS: Memphis Red Sox; NBY: New York Black Yankees; NSS: New Orleans; St. Louis Stars; NWE: Newark Eagles; NYC: New York Cubans; PDS: Philadelphia Stars; SLS: St. Louis Stars; TRU: Trujillo All-Stars

Note: These statistics are not completed nor audited. They are presented as an example of the talent of Ted Strong Jr.

NOTES

CHAPTER 1: IT STARTED WITH A SENIOR

1. Dennis Buck, *From Slavery to Glory: African Americans Come to Aurora, Illinois 1850–1920* (Aurora, IL: River Street Press, 2005), 29.
2. Buck, *From Slavery to Glory*, 25.
3. Buck, *From Slavery to Glory*, 36.
4. Sherman Jenkins, "A Tower of Strength, Theodore Strong, 83, Still an Active Leader," *Chicago Defender*, 6 August 1977, 5.
5. *McCoy's Aurora, IL City Directory*, 1910–1911, 358.
6. Millie Benson, e-mail message to author, 24 April 2003.
7. Jenkins, "A Tower of Strength," 5.
8. Jenkins, "A Tower of Strength," 5.
9. Dick Clark and Larry Lester, *The Negro Leagues Book* (Cleveland: Society for American Baseball Research, 1994), 64.
10. Ted Strong Sr., personal interview with author, 18 May 1980.
11. Jasper Strong, personal interview with author, 20 August 2013.
12. Jasper Strong, personal interview, 20 August 2013.
13. Jasper Strong, personal interview, 20 August 2013.
14. William L. Tuttle Jr., *Race Riot* (New York: Atheneum, 1974), 5.
15. Tuttle, *Race Riot*, 5–6.
16. Jasper Strong, personal interview with author, 20 August 2013.
17. Ted Strong Sr., personal interview, 18 May 1980. The Roosevelt-Bankers State Bank collapsed around 1929. Reports in the *Chicago Defender* in 1923 stated, "The condition of the Roosevelt-Bankers State bank was the most wretched of any of the institutions that closed on the South side during the past two and a half years. Immediately upon its closing private investigators began uncovering evidence of open fraud and cheating. It was not long before the state attorney's office stepped in and indictments followed quickly. . . . The 22,000 depositors who lost more

than $1,000,000 in the bank have already begun to protest against the small fine and sentence imposed on the brothers [owners]."

18. Ted Strong Sr., personal interview, 18 May 1980.

19. Ted Strong Sr., personal interview, 18 May 1980.

20. Ted Strong Sr., personal interview, 18 May 1980.

21. Ted Strong Sr., personal interview, 18 May 1980.

22. Ted Strong Sr., personal interview, 18 May 1980.

23. Ted Strong Sr., personal interview, 18 May 1980.

CHAPTER 2: "TED WAS BIG FOR HIS AGE"

1. Abe Saperstein Harlem Globetrotters Papers, *Globetrotters History Very Special Clips For Filing*, Box 2.325/P14C, Dolph Briscoe Center for American History, Austin, Texas.

2. Abe Saperstein Harlem Globetrotters Papers, *The Story of the Origin of the Harlem Globetrotters, written by Marie Linehan*, 11 November 1979, Box 2.325/P14C, Dolph Briscoe Center for American History, Austin, Texas.

3. Ted Strong Sr., personal interview with author, 18 May 1980.

4. Ted Strong Sr., personal interview, 18 May 1980.

5. Ted Strong Sr., personal interview, 18 May 1980.

6. Dempsey Travis, *An Autobiography of Black Chicago* (Chicago: Urban Research Institute, Inc., 1981), 52.

7. Travis, *An Autobiography*, 52.

8. T. R. Poston, "145,000 Protest To Roosevelt, Roosevelt Refuses To See Leaders of Large Delegation," *New York Amsterdam News*, 10 May 1933, 1.

CHAPTER 3: TED JR. COMES INTO HIS OWN

1. G. D. Lewis, "Sports Squibs," *Chicago Defender*, 6 June 1936, 14.

2. Donald Spivey, *If You Were Only White: The Life of Leroy "Satchel" Paige* (Columbia: University of Missouri Press, 2012), 123–24.

Paige was being hotly pursued by representatives of the Dominican Republic, whose leader, dictator Rafael Trujillo, was determined to have his baseball team, Ciudad Trujillo also known as the Dragones, victorious in the national championship against his political rival. The news as late as April 19, 1937, reported that team Ciudad Trujillo was advancing but was having trouble. The Dominican sports page raised the specter of possible defeat of team Ciudad Trujillo. There was a general consensus that Trujillo's team was not quite strong enough. One of the opposing teams had recruited the heralded Martin Dihigo. The Trujillo team needed strengthening if they hoped to have a chance to outclass their rivals and make it to the finals and win the best-of-seven series for the championship. . . .

Trujillo's emissary had already made an offer to one player, whom he successfully recruited for $750, and was looking to recruit others, but had to have Satchel Paige. . . .

He offered $30,000 for the master hurler's services, and that of seven other players of his choosing, in the Dominican Republic for the 1937 season. The money proved to be irresistible to Paige, who approached his catcher, William Perkins, to go with him, and then enticed Cool Papa Bell, Josh Gibson, and others to join with them. Able to offer them several thousands dollars each, and pocketing something extra for his putting together the team, it was an extraordinary payday for Paige and his Negro Leagues supporting cast.

3. Dempsey Travis, *An Autobiography of Black Chicago* (Chicago: Urban Research Institute, Inc., 1981), 80.

4. Frank A. Young, "East Trounces West in Annual Game, 7–2" *Chicago Defender*, 14 August 1937, 20.

5. Young, "East Trounces West," 20.

6. "Changes Are Made in 1938 League Race." *Chicago Defender*, 26 February 1938, 8. "The league went on record as approving an agreement with the Eastern circuit respecting player agreement. No players under suspension with a national league club will be eligible to play with an American league club or vice versa until the president or chairman of that league lifts the suspension. At the same time all contracts with club owners in one league will be respected by the other league."

CHAPTER 4: THE SKY IS THE LIMIT

1. Frank A. Young, "West Beats East in Classic Thriller, 5 To 4," *Chicago Defender*, 27 August 1938, 9.

2. Frank A. Young, "Dandridge as Good as Mel Ott at His Best . . . Third Sacker of Newark Is Given Praise," *Chicago Defender*, 24 September 1938, 9.

3. Lloyd Lewis, "'Negro Ball Is Faster' Says Lloyd Lewis," *Chicago Defender National Edition*, 27 August 1938, 8.

4. Josh Wilker, *The Harlem Globetrotters* (Philadelphia: Chelsea House Publishers, 1997), 50.

The Rens, for most people who paid attention to professional basketball, were the black team of the 1920s and 1930s. Founded in 1923 by a black immigrant from Saint Kitts in the Caribbean named Robert Douglas, the Rens had been a success from their earliest games in the Renaissance Ballroom in Harlem. Unlike the Globetrotters in the early years, the Rens made money. The Rens also differed from the Globetrotters in that, since they were based in New York City, the nation's hotbed of professional basketball at that time, they were able early on to prove their mettle against top eastern teams like the Original Celtics and the Philadelphia Sphas. . . . By 1939 the Rens had been at the top of the basketball world for longer than any team around, save for their old rivals, the Original Celtics. . . . The Rens showed no signs of decline.

5. "Rens Defeat Harlem Globe Trotters . . . N. Y. Quint Advances to Finals," *Chicago Defender National Edition*, 1 April 1939, 8.

6. Ted Strong Sr., personal interview with author, 18 May 1980.

7. Paul Debono, *The Indianapolis ABCs: History of a Premier Team in the Negro Leagues* (Jefferson, NC: McFarland, 1997), 116.

A short time later, Quincy Trouppe was on his way to a team in Monterrey, Mexico, having been recommended by "Cool Papa" Bell. Ted Strong Jr., signed with the Monarchs, and the heart of the 1938 ABCs-Blues squad was gutted. The ABCs stayed on the road, playing in Cleveland and Kansas City. There may have been a slip of paper constituting a formal relationship between Indianapolis and the Atlanta Black Crackers ("Indianapolis's Negro American League representatives"), but the 1939 NAL ABCs apparently dropped out of the league before they ever got to Indianapolis for a home game.

8. John "Buck" O'Neil, *I Was Right on Time* (New York: Fireside, 1996), 85. Buck O'Neil added, "The Monarchs didn't get back into league play until 1937, when they joined the new Negro American League, and Kansas City was glad to have them back home."

9. O'Neil, *I Was Right on Time*, 85–86.

10. O'Neil, *I Was Right on Time*, 86–87.

11. "Red Sox Defeat Monarchs 6 to 2," *Chicago Defender National Edition*, 20 May 1939, 8.

12. "Monarchs Grab 2 Games," *Chicago Defender National Edition*, 5 August 1939, 10.

13. Fay Young, "Home Runs Beat East in Baseball Classic 4 to 2," *Chicago Defender National Edition*, 12 August 1939, 1.

14. Young, "Home Runs Beat East," 1.

15. "Gibson Leads Attack as East Beats West, 7–2 [10–2]," *New York Daily Worker*, 28 August 1939.

16. "Monarchs Blank Paige's All-Stars in Two Games," *Chicago Defender National Edition*, 7 October 1939, 10.

17. Jasper Strong, personal interview with author, 9 September 2013.

CHAPTER 5: PRIME TIME ABOUNDS WITH HICCUPS

1. Ted Strong Sr., personal interview with author, 18 May 1980.

2. Matt Wyse, "Harlemites to Play Double Header Thursday . . . New Yorkers Show Marvelous Ability Against All-Stars," *The Ogden (UT) Standard-Examiner*, 26 December 1939, 8.

3. "Harlem Globe Trotters Delight Basketball Fans with Fine Show," *Helena Daily Independent*, 28 February 1940, 7.

4. "Globe Trotters '5' in National Pro Cage Tournament," *Chicago Defender National Edition*, 9 March 1940, 24.

5. "Globe Trotters '5,'" 24.

6. Josh Wilker, *The Harlem Globetrotters* (Philadelphia: Chelsea House Publishers, 1997), 51–52.

> As 20,000 fans buzzed with excitement, the trotters took a few jittery pregame warm-up shots and nervously perused their opponents. The confident Rens, garbed in flashy warm-up suits with the words "World Champions" emblazoned on the back, assaulted the basket at the other end of the court with deadeye long-range bombs and rattling slam dunks. The Globetrotters retreated to the locker room just before the game was to begin, their confidence badly shaken.

7. Abe Saperstein Harlem Globetrotters Papers, *Harlem Globetrotters 1948–1949 Edition or 22nd Year Yearbook, Story of the Harlem Globetrotters*, Box2.324/P14C. Dolph Briscoe Center for American History, Austin, Texas.

8. "Globe Trotter's Cop World Pro Cage Crown," *Chicago Defender National Edition*, 30 March 1940, 23: "The officiating was good. However, there were those who believed Ted Strong was put out of the game on fouls without good reasons—two of the five personals called against him were questioned. It was a hard blow to the sepia team when Strong was forced out. It broke up their style of play."

9. "Globe Trotter's Cop World," 23: "Bernie Price, formerly of Toledo University, let go the ball from the center of the floor. It sailed through the air and right through the basket for the two points which put the Globetrotters in the lead 31 to 29 and which won the game."

10. Timuel D. Black Jr., personal interview with author, 2 February 2014.

11. Walter Henri Dyett was the renowned band director at Wendell Phillips High School.

12. Timuel D. Black Jr., personal interview, 2 February 2014.

13. Morris Gordon, personal interview with author, 27 January 2014.

14. Fay Young, "The Stuff Is Here," *Chicago Defender*, 25 May 1940, 23: "There are many who take the side of the ball player who has aired his views on the street corners. Some clubs have been tardy in paying off the men at the end of the season. When a man works, he is at least entitled to the pay bargained for when it is due. The East vs. West game is still a nasty pill in the mouths of most of the players. Getting a ride to Chicago and expenses paid hasn't set so well with these players. They want a little something added."

15. "Globe Trotters Work Out with Sheboygan," *Chicago Defender*, 23 November 1940, 22.

16. "Globe Trotters Work Out," 22.

17. John C. Day, "College All-Stars Win 44-42 Overtime Game from Globe Trotters," *Chicago Defender National Edition*, 7 December 1940, 23.

18. Matt Wyse, "Harlemites to Battle Ogden Five . . . World Champions to Perform February 5 At Ogden High Court," *Ogden (UT) Standard-Examiner*, 26 January 1941, 8-A.

19. Wyse, "Harlemites to Battle Ogden Five," 8-A.

20. Morris Gordon, personal interview, 27 January 2014.

21. "Globetrotters' Strong Mixture of Great Stars . . . Six-Three 210 Pound Giant Has Developed Into Outstanding Performer," *Cumberland (MD) Evening Times*, 26 February 1941, 16.

22. Eddie Gant, "I Cover the Eastern Front," *Chicago Defender National Edition*, 1 March 1941, 23.

23. "N. Y. Rens, Globe Trotters Set For Pro Tourney," *Chicago Defender National Edition*, 15 March 1941, 22.

24. Timuel D. Black Jr., personal interview, 2 February 2014.

25. "Globe Trotters Visit Night Spots—And Lose," *Chicago Defender National Edition*, 29 March 1941, 23.

26. "East Vs. West Game In Chicago On Sunday, July 27 . . . Baseball Men In Session," *Chicago Defender National Edition*, 1 March 1941, 23.

What started out to be a jittery joint meeting because of the eastern owners' threat to withdraw over the return of players who jumped to Mexico and Venezuela, ended peacefully when Tom Beard, Kansas City, MO, offered a motion to amend the law placing a three-year ban on jumping players.

Beard's amendment gave the players who jumped their contract until May 1 of this year to get back to their original clubs. In the event that they fail to do so these players face a five-year suspension. Also, players who jump after May 1 or remain away are to be banned for five years.

Players who jumped are not getting back without any punishment. A fine of $100 has been slapped on them if they wish to play league baseball and this fine is to be paid into the treasury of the league.

The amendment won easily. Of the 12 owners who voted, 10 went on record for the amendment. One voted against and Abe Manley, Newark Eagles, who had held out against the return unless under the original ban, refused to vote. Following the joint session, Cum Posey, part owner of the Homestead Grays, let it be known that the Grays had already signed up Josh Gibson, ace catcher and star of the East vs. West game of 1939.

27. Janet Bruce, *The Kansas City Monarchs: Champions of Black Baseball* (Lawrence: University Press of Kansas, 1985), 92.

28. Frank Young, "Paige Routed But Kansas City Wins Opener," *Chicago Defender National Edition*, 31 May 1941, 22.

29. Larry Lester, *Black Baseball's National Showcase: The East-West All-Star Game, 1933–1953* (Lincoln: University of Nebraska Press, 2001), 1.

30. Effa Manley, "Negro League Owners Spend $480,000 Yearly," *Chicago Defender National Edition*, 19 July 1941, 24.

31. Jasper Strong, personal interview with author, 9 September 2013.

32. John C. Day, "East Trims West, 8 To 3 . . . Buck Leonard's Home Run and Pitching of Paige Feature Game," *Chicago Defender National Edition*, 2 August 1941, 1.

> Lefty Hill of Newark took the mound for the East in the eighth. The West scored two runs in the eighth with the help of some errors. Armour missed the third strike and was safe at first when Campanella dropped the ball and Armour legged it to first ahead of the throw. Strong hit to Irvin at third. Irvin tossed too late to get Armour at second and on the throw to first, Strong was safe. In the mean time Armour went to third. Bostock hit to Seay and Seay to Martinez killed Strong at second but Seay threw wild to Leonard allowing Armour to score and Bostock to reach second. Coimbre dropped Woods' fly in right, Bostock scoring and Woods going to second. Ford rolled out to Leonard unassisted.

33. "Fight Follows East-West Classic," *Chicago Defender National Edition*, 2 August 1941, 20.

CHAPTER 6: THE FIFTEENTH SEASON

1. "Kansas City Plays Newark in N.Y. On August 24," *Chicago Defender National Edition*, 23 August 1941, 24.

2. Abe Saperstein Harlem Globetrotters Papers, *Globetrotters History Very Special Clips For Filing*, Box 2.325/P14C, Dolph Briscoe Center for American History, Austin, Texas.

> Basic: $85.00
> Bonus: $10.00
> Total: $95.00
> S S: $00.95
> Net: $94.05
> 12/4/41 At New Castel, Pa 35.00
> 12/2/41 At Chicago, IL (Bag) 1.95
> 12/9/41 At Decatur, IL 10.00
> 12/11/41 At LaCrosse, Wisc. 10.00
> 12/16/41 At Aberdeen, So Dak 45.00
> Total 101.95
> S S .95
> Net 101.00
> Due 95.00
> Over Paid 6.00

3. "Trotters Hold 1st Practice," *Chicago Defender National Edition*, 15 November 1941, 22.

4. J. Russ Cowans, "Globe Trotters Stop Detroit's Brown Bombers," *Chicago Defender National Edition*, 29 November 1941, 22: "The Globe Trotters, behind in the first three periods, went into the final minute of play with a two-point deficit, but tied the count when Bernie Price slipped past the Brown Bomber defense, took a long pass from Ted Strong, and sank the basket without opposition. Larry Bleach then fouled Babe Pressley and the latter tossed in the basket to clinch the victory."

5. Dempsey Travis, *An Autobiography of Black Chicago* (Chicago: Urban Research Institute, Inc., 1981), 93–94.

6. "Globe Trotters Win from Eagles, 36-22," *Chicago Defender National Edition*, 20 December 1941, 23.

7. Travis, *An Autobiography of Black Chicago*, 94.

8. "Brilliant Cager," *Cumberland, MD Evening Times*, 18 March 1942, 16.

9. "Remains With Kansas City," *Chicago Defender National Edition*, 25 April 1942, 20: "Ted Strong, veteran outfielder and first sacker for the Kansas City Monarchs, was signed up last Friday night by Tom Baird, representing J. L. Wilkinson, owner of the Monarchs, Friday night in Chicago. Strong had not exactly been a holdout but was seriously considering the flattering offer to play with the white Grumman Flyers of Long Island, N. Y. After a half-hour conference with Baird, Strong put his 'John Henry' on the dotted line and left Saturday to report to Manager Dizzy Dismukes of the Monarchs in Monroe, La."

10. Donald Spivey, *If You Were Only White: The Life of Leroy "Satchel" Paige* (Columbia: University of Missouri Press, 2012), 186–87.

11. Eddie Gant, "I Cover the Eastern Front," *Chicago Defender National Edition*, 27 June 1942, 21.

CHAPTER 7: 1942–1943: A SEASON OF CHANGE, WORLD WAR II CALLS

1. Jasper Strong, personal interview, 20 August 2013.

2. "Baseball Season Over: No Big League Tryouts . . . Run-Around Given Negro Ball Players . . . Lots of Wild Talk, But No Action by Owners or Managers," *Chicago Defender National Edition*, 10 October 1942, 24.

3. "Studebakers Out of Pro Cage Meet . . . Minneapolis Wins in Last 29 Seconds," *Chicago Defender National Edition*, 20 March 1943, 21.

4. Ole Nosey, "Everybody Goes When the Wagon Comes," *Chicago Defender National Edition*, 27 March 1943, 12.

5. Fay Young, "Through the Years . . . Past Present Future," *Chicago Defender National Edition*, 27 March 1943, 20.

6. "Seabee History," Seabee Museum and Memorial Park, Davisville, RI, www.seabeesmuseum.com (16 May 2013).

7. "Navy Enlist Specialist on Reserve List . . . Volunteers Sought for Construction and Headquarter Unit," *Chicago Defender National Edition*, 18 July 1942, 7.

8. "Navy Enlist Specialist on Reserve List," 7.

9. "Navy Seeks Overseas Work Unit," *Chicago Defender National Edition*, 24 October 1942, 1.

> The base pay of these men will range from $54 a month to $96 for those who qualify as second class petty officers. Married men will be allowed $37.50 a month in addition for their families. All men will draw base pay plus 20 per cent while on foreign duty. Age limits are from 15 to 50 years.
>
> The battalion is to be composed of carpenters, steel workers, welders, pipe-fitters, mechanics and laborers, Lieut. Harrison said.
>
> The officer also announced a drive for those who can qualify as first class and second class petty officers for service as cooks, stewards and mess attendants. Cooks will receive base pay of $114 a month plus allowances for their families and a 20 percent increase for foreign duty.

10. "What the People Say: Sailor Blasts Bias in Navy Seabees," *Chicago Defender National Edition*, 19 December 1942, 14.

11. Jonathan D. Sutherland, *African Americans at War: An Encyclopedia, Volume Two* (Santa Barbara, CA: ABC-CLIO, 2004), 555.

> In June 1940 African Americans in the U. S. Navy made up just 2.3 percent of the population of 170,000 or 4,007 men. Of that number, 4001 were members of the stewards branch; the other 6 were regular Navy men, specifically retained in that status when changes to Navy enlistment regulations in 1922 required that all African Americans enlisting or re-enlisting in the Navy join the stewards branch. Over the next few years the African American regular Navy, except for these six, left the Navy. Although officially this policy ended in 1932, in practice the Navy did not welcome African Americans except as stewards.

12. Charley Cherokee, "National Grapevine . . . Anchors Aweigh Off," *Chicago Defender National Edition*, 6 November 1943, 15.

13. "Summary of Ranks and Rates of the U. S. Navy: Together with Designations and Insignia," *Bureau of Naval Personnel Information Bulletin*, Number 314, May 1943, 2.

14. Dr. Frank A. Blazich Jr., "Building for a Nation and for Equality: African American Seabees in World War II," Naval History Blog, U.S. Naval Institute, www.navalhistory.org (4 March 2014).

15. Fay Young, "Through the Years . . . Ted Strong in South Pacific," *Chicago Defender National Edition*, 15 September 1945, 9.

CHAPTER 8: THE BROTHERS RETURN

1. "Bernie Price, Strong Back in Globetrotters' Lineup," *Chicago Defender National Edition*, 26 January 1946, 9.

2. Fay Young, "Through the Years," *Chicago Defender National Edition*, 16 March 1946, 9.

3. Young, "Through the Years," 9.

4. John "Buck" O'Neil, *I Was Right On Time* (New York: Fireside, 1996), 87.

5. Howdy House, "Colored Stars Uncork Funfest after Building Up Big Last Half Lead," *Coshocton (OH) Tribune*, 16 March 1946, 2.

6. "George Mikan in Pro Ranks," *Coshocton (OH) Tribune*, 16 March 1946, 2: "George Mikan, America's No. 1 college basketball player, became a professional today. The six-foot, nine-inch DePaul University all-American signed to play yesterday with the American Gears of the National professional basketball league and will receive $60,000 over a five-year span, record sum for a professional basketball player."

7. Abe Saperstein Harlem Globetrotters Papers, *Harlem Globetrotters 1948–1949 Edition or 22nd Year Yearbook, Story of the Harlem Globetrotters*, Box2.324/P14C, Dolph Briscoe Center for American History, Austin, Texas.

8. Ben Green, *Spinning the Globe: The Rise, Fall and Return to Greatness of the Harlem Globetrotters* (New York: HarperCollins, 2005), 191.

9. Larry Lester, *Black Baseball's National Showcase: The East-West All-Star Game, 1933–1953* (Lincoln: University of Nebraska Press, 2001), 243.

Rickey announced that he had leased Ebbets Field to Joe Hall of the Brooklyn Brown Dodgers for five home dates. The league would debut on May 20 with the Brown Dodgers hosting the Philadelphia Hilldales. The other scheduled dates included a May 27 meeting with Greenlee's Crawfords, May 30 against Detroit, a night game on June 6 against Hilldale, and a June 17 contest with the Chicago Brown Bombers. Often called "The Mahatma," Rickey, who is credited with starting baseball's minor league system, secured other ballparks for team owners. The Pittsburgh Crawfords played at Forbes Field, Philadelphia at Harrisburg Field, Detroit at Motor City Field, Chicago at Wrigley Field, and Toledo at American Association Park. The shrewd, bow-tied, cigar-chewing Rickey was known for his priestly manner and flowery speech, which sometimes gave him the mannerisms of a con man playing Daddy Grace. He repeatedly charged that the Negro National and Negro American Leagues were unsound and not part of "organized" baseball. The Methodist teetotaler Rickey claimed the black leagues were in "the zone of a racket." However, all-star Grays first baseman Buck Leonard countered, "We were organized, just not recognized."

Meanwhile Rickey made no promises that the new league would serve to integrate Negro players in the major leagues. He emphasized that the new league would be a sound structure and, in time, be accepted by the National Association of Professional Baseball Clubs. At a press conference, Rickey refused to answer questions about whether the acceptance of the United States League by the Association would make Negro players eligible for signing with major league clubs. Quietly, club owners like Dr. Martin and Effa Manley encouraged a wait-and-see attitude toward Rickey's objectives in establishing this new all-black league. Ironically, Rickey postulated that an all-black league owned by a white American would be accepted by Major League Baseball over an all-black league with African-American ownership.

10. Kyle P McNary, *Ted "Double Duty" Radcliffe: 36 Years of Pitching & Catching in Baseball's Negro Leagues* (St. Louis Park, MN: McNary Publishing, 1994), 183.

11. John Holway, *Voices from the Great Black Baseball Leagues* (New York: Dodd, Mead, 1975), 345.

12. Alvin Spearman, personal interview with author, 3 April 2014.

CHAPTER 9: "LIFE FOR ME AIN'T BEEN NO CRYSTAL STAIR"

1. Langston Hughes, "Mother to Son," *Crisis Magazine*, 1922.

2. Fay Young, "Newark Ties Kansas in World Series," *Chicago Defender National Edition*, 28 September 1946, 11.

3. "Kansas City Takes Lead in World Series Play," *Chicago Defender National Edition*, 28 September 1946, 10.

Then Satchel Paige, who starred in a relief role in the opening game at the Polo Grounds, took over.

The Eagles pounced on Paige for three hits and three runs in the sixth. Monty Irvin, Eagles shortstop, opened the seventh with a home run drive over the 350-foot right field fence to end the scoring.

Following the game, the two clubs left for Chicago where the fifth game will be played tomorrow night at Comiskey Park. The remaining games of the best four out of seven series will be played in Newark starting Friday.

4. "Army Vet Hurls Newark to World Series Title," *Chicago Defender National Edition*, 5 October 1946. 11.

5. John "Buck" O'Neil, *I Was Right On Time* (New York: Fireside, 1996), 176–77.

Before the seventh and deciding game, we were changing in the visitors' clubhouse when Frank Duncan came in and asked, "Anybody seen Willard and Ted?" Satchel was still AWOL, but now Willard Brown and Ted Strong were missing, too. The story we got was that they had gone into New York that morning to sign winter ball contracts with the Puerto Rican League and they hadn't gotten back. Willard and Ted didn't show up until the game was almost over, saying they'd gotten caught in traffic. Satchel? He didn't show up at all.

I know this sounds crazy—I warned you that it would—but to Willard and Ted, negotiating a winter contract was more important than the ballgame, game seven or not, because they were trying to make a living, and now they knew they were going to work all winter. We also had to go with Hilton and Joe Greene, usually our catcher, in the outfield instead of Willard and Ted. All great players, but there we were, trying to play the seventh game of the World Series without Satchel Paige and two other guys I think belong in the Hall of Fame.

6. O'Neil, *I Was Right On Time*, 179.

7. "Monarch Player Quits Team; Says He Got Mad When Offered $750 Bribe," *Kansas City Call*, 11 October 1946, 10.

8. "Monarch Player Quits Team," 10.

9. "Monarch Player Quits Team," 10.

10. Fay Young, "Through the Years," *Chicago Defender*, 5 October 1946, 9.

11. Janet Bruce, *The Kansas City Monarchs: Champions of Black Baseball* (Lawrence: University Press of Kansas, 1985), 92.

CHAPTER 10: 1947

1. Fay Young, "Through the Years," *Chicago Defender*, 22 February 1947, 21.

2. Ted Strong Sr., personal interview with author, 18 May 1980.

3. Abe Saperstein Harlem Globetrotters Papers, *Harlem Globetrotters 1948–1949 Edition or 22nd Year Yearbook, Story of the Harlem Globetrotters*, Box 2.324/P14C, Dolph Briscoe Center for American History, Austin, Texas.

4. "Robinson Plays Flawless Ball with Brooklyn Dodgers Club," *Chicago Defender National Edition*, 19 April 1947, 19.

5. John "Buck" O'Neil, *I Was Right On Time* (New York: Fireside, 1996), 179.

6. Fay Young, "Big Leagues Scout 8 Negro Players," *Chicago Defender*, 2 August 1947, 1.

7. Timuel D. Black Jr., personal interview with author, 2 February 2014.

8. "Trotters Open Here Nov. 13 . . . Play Indian Quint on Stadium Court," *Chicago Defender National Edition*, 18 October 1947, 19.

9. John Christgau, *Tricksters in the Madhouse* (Lincoln: University of Nebraska Press, 2004), 5.

10. Christgau, *Tricksters in the Madhouse*, 5.

11. Christgau, *Tricksters in the Madhouse*, 15.

12. Christgau, *Tricksters in the Madhouse*, 19.

13. Christgau, *Tricksters in the Madhouse*, 15.

14. Timuel D. Black Jr., personal interview, 2 February 2014.

15. Timuel D. Black Jr., personal interview, 2 February 2014.

16. "Last Second Win by Globetrotters Gives 17,823 'Biggest' Thrill," *Chicago Defender National Edition*, 28 February 1948, 11.

17. Timuel D. Black Jr., personal interview, 2 February 2014.

18. Timuel D. Black Jr., personal interview, 2 February 2014.

19. Christgau, *Tricksters in the Madhouse*, 140.

20. Ben Green, *Spinning the Globe: The Rise, Fall and Return to Greatness of the Harlem Globetrotters* (Columbia: University of Missouri Press, 2012), 209.

21. "Goose Tatum, Strong Sign Clown Contracts," *Chicago Defender National Edition*, 20 March 1948, 11.

22. Donald Spivey, *If You Were Only White: The Life of Leroy "Satchel" Paige* (Columbia: University of Missouri Press, 2012), 223.

23. Spivey, *If You Were Only White*, 225–26.

24. "Cubans vs. Clowns at Polo Grounds . . . Face Grays in Two Games on Sunday," *Afro-American*, 17 July 1948, 7.

25. Paul Bauer and Frazier Robinson, *Catching Dreams: My Life in the Negro Baseball Leagues* (Syracuse, NY: Syracuse University Press, 1999), 75–76.

26. Jasper Strong, personal interview with author, 9 September 2013.

27. 1942 Draft Registration card, Ted Strong Sr.

28. Dempsey Travis, *An Autobiography of Black Chicago* (Chicago: Urban Research Institute, Inc., 1981), 121.

29. Christopher Manning, *The Encyclopedia of Chicago* (Chicago: University of Chicago Press, 2004), 6.

30. Philip Dodd, "Justices Bar Real Estate Racial Curb," *Chicago Daily Tribune*, 4 May 1948, 1: "Restrictive covenants are contained in deeds to property or in agreements signed by owners of adjoining property. In their various forms, they limit ownership of designated property to the 'Caucasian race' or specify that members of the 'Negro or Mongolian' races shall not own or occupy the property named in the covenants."

31. Marriage license number 2978984, County of Cook/State of Illinois, 25 April 1949.

32. Terry Ellison, telephone conversation with author, 19 August 2014.

33. Al Warden, "Patrolling the Sports Highway," *Ogden (UT) Standard Examiner*, 14 January 1950, 6.

34. "Stars for Minot," *Bismarck North Dakota Tribune*, 28 January 1950, 6.

35. Barry Swanton, *The Mandak League: Haven for Former Negro League Ballplayers, 1950–1957* (Jefferson, NC: McFarland, 2006), 1.

36. "Satch Paige Muffles Brandon Bats," *Winnipeg (Canada) Free Press*, 31 May 1950, 26.

37. "Minot Nicks Carman," *Winnipeg (Canada) Free Press*, 2 June 1950, 18: "Minot made it 5-0 in the fourth, Strong, who had singled and taken second when Dempf walked, scoring on Felde's second single of the evening. Minot completed their scoring in the fifth. Ted Strong supplying the blow that allowed pitcher Peet and Williams to cross home plate."

38. "Minot Stops Carman by One-Sided Score," *Winnipeg (Canada) Free Press*, 30 July 1950, 18.

39. "Globe Trotters Start Filming Movie Feature," *Ogden (UT) Standard Examiner*, 13 October 1950, 14A.

40. Green, *Spinning the Globe*, 246.

41. Jasper Strong, personal interview, 9 September 2013.

42. Larry Lester, telephone conversation with author, 4 June 2014.

43. Green, *Spinning the Globe*, 247.

The Globetrotter's film was so successful in the United States that it was distributed overseas, with the encouragement of the United States Information Service (USIS), which saw it as effective propaganda. In October 1953, a USIS public affairs officer in Martinique, where the film was showing, sent a memo to his Washington headquarters entitled "Commercially Distributed Film Advances USIS Objectives," urging that the film be distributed widely around the world to "enlighten members of the local populace who have been led astray by Communist depiction of the U. S. Negro as a downtrodden, persecuted, 'second-class' citizen." In a glowing review, he described particular scenes that showed Billy Townsend being welcomed in an American university, allowed to "frequent acceptable hotels," live in a modern apartment, and be offered over "$1,000 per month to play basketball."

44. Green, *Spinning the Globe*, 248.
45. Green, *Spinning the Globe*, 248.
46. Green, *Spinning the Globe*, 250.
47. Ted Strong Sr., personal interview, 18 May 1980.
48. Ted Strong Sr., personal interview, 18 May 1980.
49. "Mob Policy Stooges Fined . . . Cops Seek Names of Gang Bosses," *Chicago Defender City Edition*, 6 December 1952, 1.
50. Editorial, "Policy in Chicago," *Chicago Defender City Edition*, 16 August 1952, 10.

CHAPTER 11: TED JR.'S YOUNGER BROTHER BEGINS TO "BREAK 'EM" OFF

1. Morris Gordon, personal interview with author, 27 January 2014.
2. Morris Gordon, personal interview, 27 January 2014.
3. Morris Gordon, personal interview, 27 January 2014.
4. Morris Gordon, personal interview, 27 January 2014.
5. Morris Gordon, personal interview, 27 January 2014.
6. Morris Gordon, personal interview, 27 January 2014.
7. Morris Gordon, personal interview, 27 January 2014.
8. Morris Gordon, personal interview, 27 January 2014.
9. Morris Gordon, personal interview, 27 January 2014.
10. Alvin Spearman, personal interview with author, 3 April 2014.
11. Alvin Spearman, personal interview, 3 April 2014.
12. Alvin Spearman, personal interview, 3 April 2014.
13. "Teams Set For Game Tomorrow . . . Globetrotters, Hawaiians Announce Starting Pitchers For Colorful Exhibition at Kanawha Park," *Charleston (WV) Gazette*, 3 August 1948, 9.
14. Jasper Strong, personal interview with author, 9 September 2013.
15. "He May Be The Boy," *Kokomo (IN) Tribune*, 20 July 1950, 19.

16. Ted Bowles, "Giants, Mallards Battle to 13-Inning Tie," *Winnipeg (Canada) Free Press*, 17 July 1952, 2.

CHAPTER 12: TWILIGHT TRIPLE HEADER

1. "Saperstein's Estate Put At $2,422,335," *Chicago Sun-Times*, 23 September 1967, 44.

> Abe Saperstein, owner of the Harlem Globetrotters basketball team who died last year, left an estate of $2,422,335.
>
> An Illinois inheritance tax form filed Friday in Circuit Court showed that the bulk of the estate was in the proceeds from the sale of the Abe Saperstein Sports Enterprises at 127 N. Dearborn.
>
> The estate paid $286,255 in federal taxes and $9,959 in state inheritance taxes.

2. Alvin Spearman, personal interview with author, 3 April 2014.

3. Ted Strong Sr., personal interview with author, 18 May 1980.

4. Sherman Jenkins, "A Tower of Strength, Theodore Strong, 83, Still an Active Leader," *Chicago Defender*, 6 August 1977, 5.

5. Jenkins, "A Tower of Strength," 5.

6. Morris Gordon, personal interview with author, 27 January 2014.

7. Alvin Spearman, personal interview, 3 April 2014.

SELECTED BIBLIOGRAPHY

"100th Naval Construction Battalion: Historical Information." Naval History and Heritage Command. Washington Navy Yard, www.history.navy.mil/museums/seabee/UnitListPages/NCB/100%2 0NCB.pdf.

Black, Timuel D., Jr. *Bridges of Memory: Chicago's First Wave of Black Migration.* Evanston, IL: Northwestern University Press and DuSable Museum of African American History, 2003.

Bohlen, Carolyn Davidica. *The Unsung Heroes: A Study of the Nonformal Educational Strategies Used by Negro League Baseball Players, 1920–1960.* Dissertation, Northern Illinois University, DeKalb, Illinois, 1999.

Brashler, William. *Josh Gibson: A Life in the Negro Leagues.* New York: Harper & Row, 1978.

Bruce, Janet. *The Kansas City Monarchs: Champions of Black Baseball.* Lawrence: University Press of Kansas, 1985.

Buck, Dennis. *From Slavery to Glory: African Americans Come to Aurora, Illinois 1850–1920.* Aurora, IL: River Street Press, 2005.

Chiarello, Mark, and Morelli, Jack. *Heroes of the Negro Leagues.* New York: Harry N. Abrams, 2007.

Christgau, John. *Tricksters in the Madhouse.* Lincoln: University of Nebraska Press, 2004.

Clark, Dick, Miller, Sammy J., and Lester, Larry. *Black Baseball in Chicago.* Chicago: Arcadia Publishing, 2000.

Debono, Paul. *The Indianapolis ABCs.* Jefferson, NC: McFarland, 1997.

Drake, St. Clair, and Cayton, Horace A. *Black Metropolis: A Study of Negro Life in a Northern City, 1945.* Chicago: University of Chicago Press, 1993.

Funke, Michael. "The Chicago Studebakers: How the UAW Helped Integrate Pro Basketball and Reunite Four Players Who Made History." *Solidarity Magazine.* United Auto Workers, June 1992.

Globetrotters History Very Special Clips for Filing, Box 2.325/P14C. Dolph Briscoe Center for American History, Austin, Texas.

Green, Ben. *Spinning the Globe: The Rise, Fall and Return to Greatness of the Harlem Globetrotters*. Columbia: University of Missouri Press, 2012.

Harlem Globetrotters 1948–1949 Edition or 22nd Year Yearbook. "Story of the Harlem Globetrotters." Box2.324/P14C. Dolph Briscoe Center for American History, Austin, Texas.

Hauser, Christopher. *The Negro Leagues Chronology: Events in Organized Black Baseball, 1920–1948*. Jefferson, NC: McFarland, 2006.

Heaphy, A. Leslie. *Black Baseball and Chicago*. Jefferson, NC: McFarland, 2006.

Holway, John. *Voices from the Great Black Baseball Leagues*. New York: Dodd, Mead, 1975.

Jenkins, Sherman. "A Tower of Strength, Theodore Strong, 83, Still an Active Leader." *Chicago Defender*, 6 August 1977.

Kovach, John M. *Baseball in South Bend*. Charleston, SC: Arcadia Publishing, 2004.

Lanctot, Neil. *Negro League Baseball: The Rise and Ruin of a Black Institution*. Philadelphia: University of Pennsylvania Press, 2004.

Lester, Larry. *Black Baseball's National Showcase: The East-West All-Star Game, 1933–1953*. Lincoln: University of Nebraska Press, 2001.

Linehan, Marie. "The Story of the Origin of the Harlem Globetrotters." 11 November 1979, Box 2.325/P14C. Dolph Briscoe Center for American History, Austin, Texas.

Luke, Bob. *The Most Famous Woman in Baseball*. Washington, DC: Potomac Books, 2011.

Manning, Christopher. *The Encyclopedia of Chicago*. Chicago: University of Chicago Press, 2004.

McNary, Kyle P. *Ted "Double Duty" Radcliffe: 36 Years of Pitching & Catching in Baseball's Negro Leagues*. St. Louis Park, MN: McNary Publishing, 1994.

Moffi, Larry, and Kronstadt, Jonathan. *Crossing the Line: Black Major Leaguers 1947–1959*. Jefferson, NC: McFarland, 1994.

O'Neil, John "Buck." *I Was Right On Time*. New York: Fireside, 1996.

Paige, Leroy (Satchel). *Maybe I'll Pitch Forever*. New York: Doubleday, 1962.

Peterson, Robert. *Only the Ball Was White*. New York: Oxford University Press, 1970.

Platt, Anthony M. *The Politics of Riot Commissions*. New York: Macmillan, 1971.

Reisler, Jim. *Black Writers/Black Baseball: An Anthology of Articles from Black Sportswriters Who Covered the Negro Leagues*. Jefferson, NC: McFarland, 1994.

Ribowsky, Mark. *A Complete History of the Negro Leagues: 1884 to 1955*. New York: Carol Publishing Group, 1995.

Riley, A. James. *The Biographical Encyclopedia of the Negro Baseball Leagues*. New York: Carroll & Graf, 1994.

Robinson, Frazier, and Bauer, Paul. *Catching Dreams: My Life in the Negro Baseball Leagues*. Syracuse, NY: Syracuse University Press, 1999.

Russell, Bill. *Go Up for Glory*. New York: Berkley, 1966.

Rust, Art, Jr. *Get That Nigger Off the Field*. New York: Shadow Lawn Press, 1992.

"Seabee History." Seabee Museum and Memorial Park, Davisville, Rhode Island. www.seabeesmuseum.com.

Spivey, Donald. *If You Were Only White: The Life of Leroy "Satchel" Paige.* Columbia: University of Missouri Press, 2012.

"Summary of Ranks and Rates of the U. S. Navy: Together with Designations and Insignia." The Bureau of Naval Personnel Information Bulletin, Number 314, May 1943.

Swanton, Barry. *The Mandak League.* Jefferson, NC: McFarland, 2006.

Travis, Dempsey. *An Autobiography of Black Chicago.* Chicago: Urban Research Institute, 1981.

Trouppe, Quincy. *20 Years Too Soon.* St. Louis: Missouri Historical Society Press, 1977.

Tuttle, William L., Jr. *Race Riot.* New York: Atheneum, 1974.

Wilker, Josh. *The Harlem Globetrotters.* Philadelphia: Chelsea House, 1997.

INDEX

ABOUT THE AUTHOR

Sherman L. Jenkins is president of SLJ Communications, Inc., a digital media company and parent firm for "Tell Me Somethin' Good" or TMSG (www.tellmesomethingood.org), a digital monthly publication that covers African American life outside the city of Chicago. He has been a researcher of the Negro Leagues and specifically Ted Strong Jr. since meeting and working with Ted Strong Sr. more than thirty years ago. Mr. Jenkins is a member of the Society for American Baseball Research's Negro Leagues Committee.

Prior to becoming a full-time author, Mr. Jenkins retired from the City of Aurora, Illinois, after serving as executive director of the city's Economic Development department. He worked in economic development for twenty-five years. Before the economic development tenure, Mr. Jenkins's background was in journalism, working for newspapers such as the *Rockford Mid-West Observer* and as a freelance writer/photographer for the *Chicago Daily Defender*. Moreover, he served as director of communications for two of Chicago's largest youth-serving organizations, and as a member of Golin/Harris Communications, Inc. in Chicago, he directed and handled national public relations programs for the McDonald's Corporation.

He lives in Aurora, Illinois.